PARAC

THE SKYDIV

**By
Dan
Poynter**

". . .AND ONCE YOU HAVE TASTED FLIGHT, YOU WILL WALK THE EARTH WITH YOUR EYES TURNED SKYWARD, FOR THERE YOU HAVE BEEN, AND THERE YOU LONG TO RETURN. . ."

PARACHUTING

THE SKYDIVERS' HANDBOOK

By Dan Poynter

Published by:

Parachuting Publications
Post Office Box 4232
Santa Barbara, CA 93103, U.S.A.

Books by the author:

PARACHUTING MANUAL WITH LOG, *a basic training text.*
THE PARACHUTE MANUAL, *a technical treatise on the parachute.*
I/E COURSE, *a home study course for parachuting Instructor/Examiner candidates.*
HAND GLIDING MANUAL WITH LOG, *a basic training text.*
HANG GLIDING, *the basic handbook of skysurfing.*
MANNED KITING, *the basic handbook of tow launched hang gliding.*
HANDBUCH DES DRACHENFLIEGERS.
PARACHUTE RIGGING COURSE, *a course of study for the FAA senior rigger certificate.*
PARACHUTING, *the skydivers' handbook.*
FRISBEE PLAYERS' HANDBOOK.

Copyright © 1978 by Daniel F. Poynter

First edition

Printed in the United States of America

Library of Congress Cataloging in Publication Data.
Poynter, Daniel F., 1938-
Parachuting, The Skydivers' Handbook.
1, Parachuting. 2, Skydiving. I Title
GV 770.P69   797.56   77-83469
ISBN 0-915516-16-0 Paperback
ISBN 0-915516-17-9 Hard Cover

ABOUT THE AUTHOR

Dan Poynter is a licensed pilot, rated for both powered airplanes and gliders, an expert parachutist with all the highest licenses and ratings and a licensed master parachute rigger who began his aviation career in 1962 when he made his first jump while attending law school. In his fifteen year, 1,200 jump career he has been responsible for numerous notable equipment advances (some patented) and, perhaps even more important, the dissemination of an incredible amount of parachuting information. Many of his jumps were made to test reserve canopies, gliding wings and other deceleration devices.

He has been a member of the USPA Board of Directors since 1966 and has served as Chairman of the Safety and Training Committee, a member of the Executive Committee, as Secretary and as Chairman of the Board. He served as Equipment Inspector at the U.S. National Parachuting Championships for ten straight years while often also taking part as a competitor, training judge or President of the Jury. In 1969, he established a parachute rigging school which became world famous; much of the material in this book was developed there. He has been an Instructor/Examiner since 1964.

Gliding canopies led him to rigid gliding devices and into hang gliding; he's written four books on the subject. Appointed Flight Examiner by the U.S. Hang Gliding Association, he serves on the Board of Directors.

In 1977, after two terms as President, he was elected Président d'Honneur of the Commission Internationale de Vol Libre (Hang Gliding) of the Fédération Aéronautique Internationale, the world body which governs aviation competition and records. He is also the U.S. alternate delegate to the Commission International De Parachutisme.

Dan was the founder and ten year editor of *The Spotter,* parachuting's newsmagazine, his articles have been published in numerous periodicals in both the U.S. and abroad and he is probably best known for his column in *Parachutist* magazine, entitled Parachuting Poynters, which has appeared since 1963, Dan is one of sport parachuting's most experienced and respected leaders.

ACKNOWLEDGEMENT

For photographs, Tom Owens, Jim Baldwin, John Buckley, Chip Maury, Bill Kiehl, Dave Granger, Ralph White, Joseph Leary, Bob Sinclair, Dan Stukey, Andy Keech, Carl Boenish, Leon Riche, Mike Jenkins, Tom Schapanski, Joe Gonzales, A.W. Fisher, Bob Buquor, Chris Wentzel, Jerry Palmer, Paul Johansen, Greg Pike, Tony Gonzales, John Garrity, Bob Woodall, Bill Hallam, Fred O'Donnell, the military services, Parachutes Incorporated, and special thanks to Jerry Irwin. Others who helped were John Randall, Ron Tavalero, Diane Lindell, Karalee Canham, E. V. Spadafora, 82nd Airborne SPC, Don Grant, Jim Bates, Charlie Shea-Simonds, Bill Ottley, Mike Leeds, Laura MacKenzie, Ted Roland, Robin Kinkead, Chuck Ryan, Al Itenson, Don Stewart, Art James, Denise Doty, Curt Curtis, Norm Fraser, Nanc Gruttman, and special thanks to Scott Hamilton for technical proofing.

I sincerely thank all these fine people and I know they are proud of the part they have played in the development of the parachute, the science and the industry as well as of their contribution to this work.

**THIS BOOK IS DEDICATED
TO
SAFETY THROUGH EDUCATION**

WARNING

Whenever man leaves the ground, he risks injury and even death. Whether to accept or reject this risk and its accompanying challenge must be a personal decision; one must weigh the risk and the reward.

This is not a do-it-yourself text. The information contained here is intended as an introduction to the sport and as a source reference. After reading this book, visit one or more of the firms listed herein for further information and instruction.

**YOUR PARACHUTING INSTRUCTOR WILL BE HAPPY
TO EXPLAIN ANY AREA OF THIS BOOK
WHICH ISN'T CLEAR TO YOU.**

TABLE OF CONTENTS

Tree landings.
Water landings, unintentional.
Powerline landings.
Other obstacles.
Airport safety.
Basic Safety Regulations.

Your freefall progression.
Class "A" License.
Ripcord pulls.
Using instruments.
Freefall tables.
Stability and body positions.
Frog position.
Back to earth.
Delta.
Aerial maneuvers.
Tracking.
Turns.
Barrel Rolls.
Forward loop.
Back loop.
Other positions and maneuvers.
Door exits.
Relative work.
Spotting.
Canopy relative work.

Major components.
Pilot chute.
Bridle.
Deployment devices; sleeves, bags, etc.
Risers.
Canopies; round, PC class, wing and ram air.
Reserve canopies.
Mid-air reserve modifications.
Harness.
Container.
Ripcord.
Ripcord pocket.
Static line.
Hardware.
Instruments.
Automatic openers.
Personal equipment; jumpsuits, helmets, etc.
Fitting the parachute assembly.
Equipment ("pin") check.
Packing; straightening, inspecting, rigging.
Parachute handling.

This is a letter from a first jump student to her friend. It relates the student's side of the initial training better than any experienced instructor could. (Reprinted from *Parachutist* magazine.)

. . . **Let me tell you** *about my latest hobby – Sky Diving! I think I probably told you ages ago that I was trying to muster up the courage to start, well I have.*

I finally screwed my courage to the sticking place and rolled along to class.

The first night was fine, it was all theory. It started out with a guy telling us that a parachute was the safest piece of equipment known to man and then spent 2½ hours telling us about all the things that can go wrong and what to do about them! A thoroughly frightened girl rolled back home again but turned up the next night for some of the practical work which included learning how to do a proper parachute landing fall (or PLF) and a practice of emergency procedures in a suspended harness. PLFs are first practiced on the ground; just try falling over in one fluid line touching the ground with your calf, thigh, buttock and shoulder. Being a fairly athletic person you might manage it. I, who hadn't done anything more strenuous than lift a drink in years found it sheer, unadulterated agony. I was aching by the time the instructor (a cold-hearted bastard if I ever met one) decided that we would go on to repeating the exercise from a four foot platform. By this time a whole lot of muscles I never knew I had were beginning to complain, after two hours of jumping off that platform they were not only complaining, they were mounting protest marches accompanied by brass bands playing the "Star Spangled Banner." I found myself unable to climb up the ladder onto the platform let alone fall off it and not add yet another bruise to what I already knew was going to be a most impressive collection.

Just when I was determined to knock myself out on the next jump the guy called for a break (working the same principle as torturers of letting their victim almost die and then letting them rest up just long enough for a spark of life to return).

During the break, one of the guys there asked what had prompted me to try sport parachuting, since the only girls he had known who tried it were girls whose boyfriends were jumpers. With a gay, brittle, insouciant laugh I replied that I thought it might be a bit of a giggle. Then comes this lugubrious voice from my instructor, "Yea, I've been laughing ever since you arrived." Encouraging bastard!

However, no rest for the wicked, out again we were forced to go through the emergency release procedures in a suspended harness. This involved climbing up a little ladder, getting strapped into a harness standing there until the Man, almost with studied insolence, kicks away the ladder and you just dangle there (shades

CHAPTER I
JUMP? OUT OF AN AIRPLANE?

Sport parachuting is fun! Skydiving is not just falling, it is flying; the closest we have been able to come to free, unencumbered, non-mechanical individual flight. Nearly everyone flies in their dreams; the young idolize Superman while the old admire the birds. Anyone who has sprung from the 3 meter board, jumped from the hayloft into a haystack or even stood on a hill in a high wind with arms outstretched has experienced a form of flight. Skydiving, individual and group flight, is what this book is all about.

Since parachuting began to catch on as a sport in the late fifties, it has become a well organized, widely recognized form of aviation activity and is now an established recreational pursuit.

Just as airline travel has changed dramatically since its beginnings back in the 1920's, sport parachuting has become an enjoyable and widely practiced activity for thousands of people who have little else in common. Advances in techniques and equipment have made the sport safe and thoroughly fun.

A sport jumper wears a highly maneuverable main parachute that lets him down so softly that he can easily stand up. He wears protective clothing: a helmet, boots, a jumpsuit, and perhaps goggles and gloves. And he wears a reserve parachute for the same reason you use a seat belt in your car — for protection in that rare case when something goes wrong.

After the jumper suits up, he climbs aboard the aircraft with fellow parachutists for a ride to thousands of feet above the ground. The higher you go, the longer is your freefall. (A common freefall time is 30 seconds, starting from 7200 feet or 2200 meters.)

Once the aircraft reaches the planned altitude, the parachutist directs the pilot to fly the plane over the proper point on the ground so that the jumper can land on target. Then out he goes!

After leaving a perfectly good airplane, the jumper accelerates for eleven seconds until he reaches some 120 mph and "terminal velocity": that speed at which his weight equals his wind resistance.

Does it feel as if he's falling? No — it's more like flying.

"Parachuting is an adventure . . . A rousing adventure which is as thrilling and challenging and rewarding as any sport yet known to any age" – Russ Gunby

of Tom Dooley). An instructor on the ground calls out various malfunctions that you might be faced with and you go through the corrective procedure. There are some types of malfunctions for which you have to get rid of the malfunctioning parachute and pull the emergency parachute ripcord. Getting rid of the main involves uncapping a couple of metal plates protecting the release rings, pulling the release rings and upon dropping away pulling the reserve.

There I am, dangling in the breeze with aching muscles, bruises coming up all over my body in most tender spots (I just knew I wasn't going to be good for anything . . . for weeks) and a whole crowd of guys who had already been through all this watching with interest – knowing full well what would happen.
The instructor calls out a particular type of malfunction for which I have to cut away and I start to go through the procedure, come the moment when I pull the release rings to get rid of the main parachute and only one of them works! I swing round in a small circle and dangle there by one strap – to the great delight of all the S.O.B.'s sitting on the ground watching.

"Don't just hang there, woman," calls out my instructor/ tormentor – for whom by now I have conceived a blind, murderous passion – "Grab it and pull hard." (I know that by now you are there ahead of me as to what I would have liked to have grabbed and pulled HARD.)

O.K. Pull, the man said, so I use both hands and the thing releases, I collapse in a heap on the ground and just lie there wishing, nay praying, that the ground would open up and I would fall through to discover myself on some warm beach in Australia.

I lie there and realize that the crowd is laughing more than the sight of me falling in an inelegant heap warrants. I look up and my instructor comes up, lays his hand on my shoulder and whispers softly to me "Lady, you're dead!" YOU FORGOT TO PULL YOUR RESERVE!"

Thankfully I lay back: if I was dead that meant I could just lie there on the nice soft green grass. Unfortunately that didn't work either. The harness had a number of straps attached to it and I was unceremoniously hoisted up by one and forced by that sadistic brute to get back up there and go through the whole thing all over again. What I felt for Pansy-Petunia, my fairy riding ground instructor by now can be regarded as sheer love compared to what I feel for my jumping instructor.

Anyhow, to cut what might be a long story short, I managed – by being forced to back for an extra night's torture – to be told I could jump on Saturday. Quite frankly at that point I would have been the happiest girl in the world if they had told me there was no way they were going to let me jump, but alas, no such luck. I

Although he reaches 120 miles per hour (190 KPH) or even 200 mph in a dive, he merely feels the pressure of the air against his body. It is a simple matter to use that air pressure to perform loops and rolls and even to "track" over the ground. Experienced jumpers frequently exit the airplane with fellow jumpers and, by maneuvering their bodies, join up to form countless formations; and they still have time to move away from each other to open their parachutes in uncrowded sky.

After checking his altimeter, the jumper ends his freefall by pulling his ripcord at 2500 feet (750 M). A rustle of nylon and a tug at the shoulders — and then there is astounding silence as the parachutist hangs beneath a multi-colored canopy for the two minute ride. The ground below is a panorama of color.

As the falling parachutist pulls his ripcord and deploys the 28 foot, flat circular canopy, he increases his ten square feet of air resistance with approximately 616 square feet of nylon cloth. This upside down cup-shaped canopy offers maximum resistance (drag) as it descends through the air at approximately 17 feet per second (5.5 MPS). Both the forward and downward free fall motion are checked by the parachute's opening.

The main parachute has forward speed and maneuverability that the jumper controls by pulling on a steering line in either hand. By taking advantage of his canopy's performance, the parachutist can steer himself precisely to his landing spot. Landings within a 20 meter circle are routine, and an experienced jumper can touch a 10 centimeter disc, even in a stiff breeze. Many landings end with a soft standup.

Landings are like hopping off a cable car, or if you're not from San Francisco, like jumping off the hood of a car moving slowly at 3 to 5 mph. Not hard but tricky because of the horizontal movement produced by the wind and forward motion of the canopy. Parachuting isn't as rough and tumble as its Army Airborne heritage would lead you to believe.

It must be remembered that the combat-scarred airborne trooper jumping into battle is only using the parachute as transportation; for him it is the fastest, safest and simplest way down. His physical conditioning prepares him for the mission which begins after the jump. Sport parachuting is considerably easier, anyone can fall.

Without adequate initial training, proper equipment, and safe jumping procedures, the sport could be dangerous, and during its early phases, it WAS dangerous. But just as flying has been made safe, new and modern equipment, improved techniques, and adequate instruction and supervision have eliminated every major cause of danger to the sport parachutist.

Over 30,000 parachutists make over two million jumps each year in North America alone with very few serious injuries.

Like other action sports, parachuting is not wihout its "routine" minor injuries, however, the majority among sport parachutists are incurred during deviations from accepted safe jumping practices.

There are some 500 parachute centers across North America and the jumping everywhere is under the control of about 300 Area Safety Officers appointed by the national organizations. Jumpmasters and instructors are licensed by the USPA and CSPA (in Canada) after undergoing rigorous training and testing sessions. Parachutists may pack their own main parachutes but mains to be used by others and all reserve parachutes must be packed only by Federally licensed parachute riggers.

Parachutists have been competing for over 50 years — since, in fact, the Cleveland

---

"I'm a coward. And I'm the first one to admit it. It scares me. Everytime . . . it scares me. But I think we like to be scared. Good and scared . . . and come out of it."

went home on Friday night and my boyfriend had a lovely evening giving vent to his sadistic tendencies by pounding me with horse embrocation in an attempt to stop my muscles from seizing up altogether.

Saturday morning I drive out to the airport, some 50 miles away, all by myself as my boyfriend has announced that he does not approve of what I'm trying to do and wants nothing to do with it; he does not even in fact want to hear about any of it. I felt a bit like the condemned man must do walking his last 200 yards – in my case I remember each of the 50 odd miles with incredible clarity, the sights, the smells, the sounds, everything. I spent several minutes reviewing all the past loves of my life surrounded by great clouds of nostalgia and finally arrived at the airport feeling quite mellow. There I was most unceremoniously dressed up in a set of overalls, glamorous boots (ugh!), and a helmet on top of which went miles of harness, a main parachute, and a reserve. At this point I felt like a cross between the Michelin man and a Dalek and just couldn't procrastinate any further by asking to go to the john! (A procedure which would have meant asking for help with getting all unstrapped – humiliating!) With the original sinking heart I followed the instructor and another student jumper out to the plane where I almost gave up for the third time that morning (What, me go up 3,000 feet in that thing? It doesn't look safe.)

My pet sadist insisted that I be first out despite my protests that I was a convinced lady libber and saw no reason for women to be accorded false courtesy. I was just told to quit bitching and get in. It took the jumpmaster hauling on me from behind and the pilot pulling from in front to get me into the plane as I was not only encumbered by the bloody great parachute but inexplicably, my legs had totally refused to function. Whether this was a result of the punishment I had taken over the last few days or just sheer funk I'll never know. With me sitting praying to all the saints and angels the plane wobbled into the air. My suddenly remembering that my library book was overdue and I had to go return it didn't even merit a comment other than a grim muttering about there being only one way I was leaving the aeroplane . . .

We got up to the height from which I was going to jump, by this time I was so scared that even my tormentor was taking pity on me and making soothing noises. Either that or he didn't know how he was going to get the other student out of the plane if I jammed up in the door and refused to move!

Well, there we are. "Get in the door," he says, this means I have to swing my legs out of the open door of the plane and wait there until we are over the drop zone. I swing my legs out (not strictly accurate, the pilot and jumpmaster push them out for they have again refused to move), the wind almost whips them off at the hips. The pilot cuts the engine – this to reduce the prop blast – and the guy says to me "Get on the step." This means I have to

Air Races in the 1920's. Today, competitions range in size and scope from local "fun" meets to regional meets and from the National Parachuting Championships to the World Parachuting Championships with over 40 participating countries. The sport is also popular at the collegiate level, where the National Collegiate Parachuting League, an affiliate of the USPA, sanctions local meets and conducts an annual championship meet that draws competitors from over 50 colleges and universities across the nation.

Not everyone competes because, as in other sports, many participants enjoy the sport without the pressures of competition.

You're probably not much different from the thousands of other newcomers to the sport who find parachuting a terrific new adventure and a lot of fun! Today's weekend sport parachuting enthusiasts come from almost every station in life. For example, there are doctors, lawyers, government officials, engineers, pilots, business men, policemen, plumbers, mechanics, housewives, secretaries, servicemen, students, and many more. They all come out on the weekend to share a great common experience. There is no one classification, not even in physical condition. There are jumpers with one leg and some with no legs, with one eye and, yes, even blind. They start at 16 years, the minimum age, and go through their 80's. About a quarter of the experienced jumpers have prior military jump experience and more than 10% are female.

Since sport parachuting began to grow twenty years ago, skydivers have racked up a lot of experience and some interesting statistics. In the U.S. 1,100 have been awarded their Gold Wings for completing 1,000 jumps, over 6,000 have qualified for the Class D Expert Parachutist License, 48 have over 3,000 jumps and 3 have crossed the 5,000 jump mark. Jumpers also record their seconds of freefall time. So far, almost 250 have been awarded the 12 Hour Freefall Badge, a dozen have crossed 24 hours and one has even managed 36 for 1½ days of skydiving.

Sport parachutists often band together into small clubs for both economic and operational reasons. Most of these 500 groups may be found at small airports around the country. Also, because of the rapid expansion of the sport, many permanent commercial sport parachute centers, similar to ski centers, have been established to cater to public parachuting needs.

To contact your nearest sport parachuting operation, consult the listings in the Appendix of this book. They are in ZIP Code order to make it easy. Since the sport is growing rapidly, there are some new drop zones which aren't listed so look in the Yellow Pages of the telephone directory under "parachutes" and/or call the nearest Federal Aviation Administration facility under "U.S. Government, Transportation, Department of". Or you may write to the national organization for a directory (see Appendix). If you live in a metropolitan area, there are probably a couple of jump operations within easy driving distance. They won't be in the middle of town because there isn't any room to land there.

Students undergo a thorough half day training session to acquaint them with the equipment, the exit procedure, canopy steering, landings, emergency procedures, etc. Some of the training is indoors in a classroom and some is outside with various pieces of training equipment. The instruction, equipment rental (which includes its packing), airplane ride, liability insurance, jumpmaster fees, etc. are all included in the first jump course at about $75. Subsequent jumps are much less.

The insurance covers personal liability and property damage and covers you in case you descend into the spectator area or damage a fruit tree. USPA and CSPA provide

---

"Why would anyone want to jump out of a perfectly good airplane?"

grab the wing strut and pull myself out of the plane doorway and balance on the jump step waiting for the command "GO." This I do, because by now I'm so scared I no longer even remember what I am doing. Seriously, I don't remember getting out there the first time, I only know I must have done it because I remember balancing there thinking "Am I never going to get the go signal?" When it came – a slap of the butt and a shouted "GO!" it was such a relief that I jumped off backwards (as prescribed) without any hesitation (anything to get off that damn step!)

I then really blew everything. The thought flashed through my mind, "What the hell am I doing?" the realization that I was falling through space followed instantaneously and my instinctive reaction – out of sheer terror – was to curl up into a fetal position. Totally the wrong thing to do as I was later unceremoniously told, at that point though I wasn't all that concerned, I had got down and that was all that mattered.

However, before I had time to do any damage the parachute opened, and I was pulled up short. This has to be the most tremendous sensation going, the first thing that struck me was the quiet. It was timeless and spaceless and a brief glimpse of a totally undemanding eternity. For a few moments – before I had to start worrying about my landing – I had some sensations that I have never had before, a total bodily involvement in a medium that was not my most tremendous high. People have all sorts of ways to "get off," to experience that extra kick from life.

I've found my thing; I'm hooked.

this insurance coverage as part of their membership; this is one of the major benefits in joining.

The first five jumps (minimum) are with a static line which activates the parachute automatically. From there you go to short delays and progress to longer ones at 5 second increments from higher and higher altitudes. Your second static line will run less than $20 if you make it the same day and many students do. Many drop zones also offer a block of jumps in a package at an attractive price.

You will learn to pack with the first class either just before or just after the first jump course and once you are signed off to pack your own main, you will save the packing charge which is often $5.

By the time you reach 20 second delays and are doing your own spotting (selecting the exit point), you will be signed off again and will no longer require a jumpmaster. And you'll probably have purchased your gear by now saving the rental fees. Like skiing, parachuting is cheaper when you own your own equipment. Experienced jumpers pay $4 to $10 per jump depending upon the altitude they want. They will spend from $200 to over $1000 for equipment depending upon whether it is new or used, plain or fancy.

For many parachuting students, their first jump is also their first airplane ride and it is for this reason that many instructors will encourage you to take an observation ride first. You'll wear a parachute and will be strapped in with a seat belt right next to the door so that you can see the jumpers leave. In fact, they may have to crawl over you to get out the door.

Your licensed instructor will give you a thorough briefing in a classroom lecture and then you will go to the outdoor training area to practice parachute landing falls (PLFs), aircraft exits and emergency procedures.

Sign up

FIRST JUMP COURSE

1 LECTURE
2 EXIT CLASS
3 LANDING CLASS
4 EMERGENCY CLASS
5 EQUIPMENT ISSUE
6 THE JUMP
7 CRITIQUE & CERTIFICATE

Course overview

Lecture

Exit class

> *"Apparently man has a need to have that hollow elevator feeling in his stomach when he straps a helmet on"* – Mike Truffer

Emergency procedure

Canopy steering

Tree landing procedure

Parachute landing falls from a one meter platform

High wind recovery and equipment familiarization

When making your static line jumps, beginning with the first or the second, you will be making a DRCP or "dummy ripcord pull". As you make your exit and go through your count, you will extract a ripcord handle from its pocket. Instead of a cable and pins, it has a brightly colored "flag" so the jumpmaster can see it as you fall away from the jump plane. If you make a good DRCP on three successive jumps, you will go on to freefall on number six. Your instructor will try to schedule you so that your last static line and your first freefall jumps are on the same day.

Into freefall, you will be making longer and longer delays, a minimum each of three 5's, (seconds), 10's, 15's, and 20's. You will go higher and higher, delaying longer and longer and always pulling the ripcord at 750 meters (2500').

During your entire student career, you will be under the direct supervision of a rated instructor or jumpmaster. You will keep a logbook and your jumpmaster will help you to write in all the particulars from each jump. For you, the log will be a great source of pride, something you will keep and cherish forever. For the jumpmaster, it will be a reference so that he can refresh his memory and monitor your progress.

Once you begin your parachuting training, your progress will be limited only by your initiative and your wallet. It is highly recommended that you digest this manual prior to the first jump course, it will place you far ahead of your classmates. Once you begin jumping, don't take any weekends off, make two or three jumps per day and take 2 weeks leave from work if you can. Gaps in training require retraining and this means lost time.

After a couple of weeks into parachuting you will find that it is more than an experience, more than a sport. It is a way of life. To some it's recreation, to others an adrenalin rush and to many it becomes a total involvement, an all encompassing, personal committment to the exclusion of every other activity. It's addictive and contagious. It becomes more important than even the basic necessities of food and sleep. An analogy may be drawn with falling in love except that in skydiving, the honeymoon is never over.

You will note as you read that measurements are given interchangably in english, metric and navigational figures and you will encounter the same situation on the drop zone. Altitude is usually given in feet, wind speed in knots, landing measurements in meters, descent speed in feet per second, climb rate in feet per minute, etc. Because of international competition, the sport of parachuting converted to metric some time ago, placing us ahead of our national governments and the aviation industry here in North America. In this text, most measurements are provided in two sets of figures and many of the conversions are approximate. For further help, consult the conversion chart in Chapter two.

This manual is designed as a basic handbook, a training text to be used in conjunction with your first jump course. If there is anything here you do not understand, ask your instructor or jumpmaster. That's what they're there for.

After the classroom lecture and the outdoor training, you will:

Strap on your gear

Receive an equipment check

Board the aircraft

Exit

Open

Steer for the landing area

And share this once in a lifetime, great experience with your instructor, fellow students and anyone else who will listen.

Make a parachute landing fall

Then you'll receive a post jump critique and your first jump certificate.

CHAPTER II
YOUR FIRST JUMP

The next step is the big one. Now that you have completed your ground training, both classroom and practical, you're ready for that long lonely leap. In some ways it is probably unfortunate that the jump won't be as great a thrill as you expected it to be. After a reading of this chapter and a thorough first jump course, it will all seem so simple, more like your second jump than your first; as though you have been here before. But this familiarity only reflects your understanding and mastery of the basics of sport parachuting which are essential ingredients for safe, enjoyable jumps. It is the purpose of your ground training to duplicate as closely as possible what you will find in the air. Yes, the best surprise is no surprise, particularly in parachuting.

Now that you have completed all the necessary preliminaries, you will be issued your parachutes, two of them: a back pack "main" and a chest pack "reserve". If you weren't wearing a jumpsuit, helmet and boots for the first jump course or if this instruction took place on another day, you'll get them now too. Your jumpmaster, who may or may not also be your instructor, will help you into the 14 kg (30 lbs.) of well engineered nylon. Most of the weight hangs heavily on the back and tugs at the shoulders as it grips you tightly. It makes you somewhat clumsy as you move about and reminds you what life would be like if you were overweight.

No doubt, you and your classmates have been manifested for a separate student flight so your jumpmaster will be the only experienced jumper on board. (Later in your jump career, you'll share the lift with other parachutists of varying levels.) Your jumpmaster will line you up on the flight line for the equipment check. This is where jumping begins to seem sort of military and, indeed, many of sport parachuting's training and jump techniques have been adapted from the armed services. The equipment check is the final visual and physical inspection made by the jumpmaster on all parachutists prior to boarding the aircraft. It is sometimes referred to as the "pin check" but since many of the newer parachutes are being designed without pins, people in the future may be hard pressed to determine the origin of the term. The check is a systematic inspection of the entire parachutist both front and rear, from top to bottom. If for any reason the flight is delayed, the check will be made again. The jumpmaster will present himself for a check by another experienced jumper. Obviously, one has to know what to look for when making the check so there is a complete discussion of it in the equipment chapter.

The pilot and jumpmaster work as a team with the pilot being primarily responsible for the aircraft and the jumpmaster taking charge of the contents. While technically, even legally, the pilot is captain of the ship, they must and do work together. Student lifts are pretty routine so the planning is not complex. Your jumpmaster may give you a last minute briefing on the wind direction and speed as well as a little pep talk.

Most jump aircraft are high-winged Cessnas carrying three to four jumpers and a pilot.

Jumps can and have been made from just about every aircraft and airplane but some are much more suitable than others. Since the object of the plane ride is to get up in order to come down, a high wing model will offer greater visibility in the direction which interests us most. Low-wing airplanes not only limit visibility, they do not offer exit aids such as a wing strut to grip and a wheel to stand on. Most parachute operations use high-winged Cessnas carrying three to four jumpers and a pilot. The single-engined monoplane will have all seats but the pilot's removed and will be otherwise stripped out for jumping. Upholstery provides comfort you won't be needing and jump gear tears it up quickly anyway. Like extra instruments and even fuel, it contributes to the weight of the overall flying machine and it is uneconomical to carry it up to altitude on a short flight only to bring it back. You may jump from a low-winged monoplane such as a Piper Cherokee 6 or even a helicopter if you are in a military sport parachute club. If so, you will receive special instruction in boarding and exits. The aircraft will be prepared for jumping by taping up any sharp objects and removing protrusions (such as handles) which could snag your gear, especially near the door. The door will either be removed or refitted with a model with hinges on the top, to permit opening and closing in flight.

When the airplane arrives, follow the commands of your jumpmaster. Always approach a plane from the rear. If you are suddenly reminded that you need something from your car, walk around the tail of the aircraft. Spinning propellers are difficult to see, particularly in all this excitement and they are very efficient meat slicers. And, incidentally, if you really love your dog and your rug rats, leave them home; an airport is no place to romp and play. Smoking isn't allowed around fuel laden aircraft or the pumps and right now you have other more important, exciting things to occupy your time.

Your jumpmaster will probably run the class through some last minute practice exits from the aircraft itself. It is a good training review and serves to refresh you on the commands to expect.

You will load the aircraft in the reverse order of exit. This may be in a random manner or the jumpmaster may place the heaviest students forward to improve the flight characteristics of the plane. Some jumpmasters like to put the girl out first on

"Skydiving: the highest speed reached in a non-mechanical sport" — Guinness's Book of World Records.

the theory that her male classmates won't dare to climb back in the door once on the step. The jumpmaster will be boarding last.

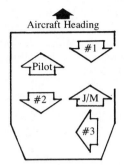

Typical Cessna seating arrangement. The jumpmaster dispatches the students in the order shown.

In a large aircraft, your static line probably won't be hooked up until the plane has climbed to 350m (1,000') or until just before your jump. But most jumpmasters prefer to hook up their students before cramming them into a small jump ship.

For your own piece of mind, yank on the static line to check its security.

Guarding and routing the static line, the jumpmaster will help you into your seating area. The parachutes are heavy, especially the back one, and tend to pull you backwards when you sit down. You are inclined to lay back and relax as best you can but you should be sitting upright. Lounging takes up more precious floor space and brings your bottom pin or breakcord tie in contact with the seat runners, etc. This could cause the main to open in the aircraft which is troublesome, expensive and sometimes dangerous. Another good reason for sitting up straight is that it will be easier to get up when the time comes.

THE RIDE UP: aircraft routine procedures.

A. Helmet secure, seat belt on, keep movement to a minimum. Movement alters the C.G. of the airplane making it more tiring to fly.

B. Cover and guard the reserve and its ripcord. An unintentional activation of the reserve parachute in the aircraft presents a hazardous situation.

C. Hold and guard the routing of your S-folded static line.

Your static line will be routed over the shoulder farthest from the door, S-folded to take up the slack and placed in your right hand. Your left arm should be placed across your reserve with your hand holding the ripcord handle firmly in place. Until you are completely out the door, your two most important responsibilities are to guard your static line and your reserve handle. Monitor your classmates to make sure they have both hands full too.

The Federal Aviation Administration requires that seat belts be provided for all passengers. However, your jump center may not buckle them up and there are some very good arguments for leaving them on the floor. Normally they are attached to the air frame just where they were before the seats were removed and this places everyone and their gear too far back for optimum weight and balance. Additionally, they are secured across the lap, under the reserve making the buckle very difficult to locate in an emergency. In a takeoff crash, those in the rear might be trapped by those in the front who are trying to find the buckle. If you are sitting by the open door, you'll feel more secure with, and should wear, the belt. If the plane has an in-flight swing up door and it's Winter, the pilot will close it now. If the weather is hot, he'll wait until just before takeoff. All of you are pretty close by now; it's tighter than a phone booth jamming contest.

The pilot starts the engine and taxies out to the end of the runway. Turning the plane away from the runway, he locks the wheels and gives the engine some gas making it roar. He glances over the many instruments and checks the mags. Satisfied the ol' jump ship is good for at least one more flight, he spins it around on the active runway and rams the throttle home. In most planes, it helps if everyone leans forward. There is so much dense cargo that just a small bit of forward shifted weight makes a big difference. After takeoff when the pilot raises the notch of flaps, reduces power and trims out for climb, you can sit back.

Your jumpmaster will probably try to add to your education and, at the same time, occupy your otherwise nervous mind by bringing a number of interesting things to your attention. If you are like many first jump students this may be your first ride in a small plane or even any aircraft. For you, this is a never before seen sight and it's particularly exciting. Look for the altimeter in the instrument panel or the one your jumpmaster is wearing. At 200' (most U.S. aircraft haven't gone metric), take a look outside at the ground so you'll recognize how close it will look later, during your parachute descent, when it's time to turn into the wind for landing. Locate the target and any areas you were told to avoid in class. Some DZs have a "bad farmer" who keeps the gear brought on to his property by trespassers. Find the pond, the power-lines, the road; get oriented. Now which way is the wind blowing? Look at the wind sock. Keep your movement in the plane to a minimum or you'll wear out the pilot. The aircraft must be balanced or the pilot has to correct with the controls. Imagine driving your car with a soft front tire, it would pull to one side and you would have to apply constant pressure to the steering wheel to keep the car straight. But the pilot has an adjustable trim tab to relieve this pressure and he'll be adjusting it to compensate for your every move. Relax and enjoy the view. Your ride up will take around ten minutes.

The seat belts come off at 1,000'. Unbuckle yours, slide the hardware to the end of the strap and lay it on the floor as far from the door as possible. A metal tipped seat belt trailing out the door may chip the paint or make a dent.

Unless this flight followed the previous lift by just a few minutes, the jumpmaster will be preparing to drop a wind drift indicator, a piece of weighted crepe paper measuring 25 cm by 6 m (10" X 20') and designed to fall at the same rate as a jumper under an open canopy. He will use it to determine the exit point. Wind varies in speed and direction at various levels. It may be calm on the ground and blowing

---

"You already know parachuting is fun. Don't worry about it; think about it. Don't guess about it; find out about it. Don't fumble around; practice. And hang around that drop zone. You don't learn about parachuting by talking (or bragging) to your whuffo friends." — George Wright

briskly at jump altitude. With accurate (which way and how much) information, he'll be able to select the best place for your exit so that you'll drift into the target area. There will be a detailed explanation of "spotting" in a later chapter but here is what you will experience the first time. At 750m (2500'), the pilot will turn approximately into the wind according to his best guess, fly across the DZ and open the door. The jumpmaster will look out and down relaying corrections to the right and left and then will throw out the wind drift indicator as the aircraft passes over the target. Banking slightly to the right, the pilot will continue to guide the aircraft in its climbing turn while the jumpmaster keeps the indicator in sight. During the next two and a half minutes the streamer will become smaller and harder to see as it descends closer to nature's camouflaged terrain. Noting the distance and direction from the target, your jumpmaster will select an exit point an equal distance upwind of the target.

Some clubs teach their students to spot right from the first jump as it keeps their mind occupied, off the worries of the jump, and gives them more confidence and a feeling of being useful. Some other operations start spotting practice on the second jump and many wait until the tenth jump or so.

As you near 850m (2800') on base leg and are about to turn onto jumprun, your jumpmaster will relieve you of your handfull of static line, pointing out the target, exit point and wind line. If you are using an automatic opener, he will arm it at this point. Press the left forearm firmly against the front of the reserve and hold the ripcord handle tightly in place to contain the canopy if the unit accidently fires during arming.

After turning on jumprun, the pilot will reach over and unlatch the swing up door. The wind will pull it open, holding it snugly up against the underside of the wing. The jumpmaster will stick his head out as the jump ship flies upwind crossing the target and heading for the exit point. He may give the pilot some slight course corrections either verbally or with hand signals. You'll notice the buffeting, cool wind, the noise and smell of the engine and it will be hard to hear. At this point, your jumpmaster may give you a little pep talk and review of the essentials: "Protect your reserve handle and your static line as you move about the aircraft. Take your time — I'll do the rest. Remember as you climb out: left foot, left hand, right foot, right hand. When you're set with your feet firmly planted and have a good grip, look in at me. When I slap you and yell 'GO', I want to see a hard arch. Look up and keep your eyes on me and your position will be good. We'll be listening for your count so you'll have to shout as loud as you can. Don't be afraid to pull the reserve if you only *think* it may be necessary. And don't forget to face into the wind, today that means toward Mount Hamilton, on landing. Think and make it a good one. See you on the ground". Or, his last minute advice may consist of just a few words. It's largely a matter of individual style.

Jumprun. The jumpmaster and pilot are busy with last second details such as assuring you a good spot.

"*Never in my life can I remember such a feeling of accomplishment*" — Michèle Gratton.

In the door. The wind will probably blow your feet away from the step.

Just before you cross the target, about ten seconds from exit, your jumpmaster will give you the first exit command: "SIT IN THE DOOR!". Swing your legs out while continuing to guard your reserve ripcord handle and visually monitoring the routing of your static line. If it snakes under the arm, you'll get a rude awakening when you reach the end of it. Also watch your jumpmaster's ripcord handles, don't knock them out. Leave some room in the doorway so your jumpmaster can peer over your shoulder at the exit point. Once you are clear of the door, you may release your grip on the reserve and grasp the wing strut with your left hand and the edge of the door with your right. It will be very windy in the prop blast. Do not at any time use the hand strap which may be over the door; they pinch fingers. It will be difficult to place your feet on the step because of the wind blast.

About three seconds prior to exit, the jumpmaster will yell "cut" and the pilot will throttle back the engine, the noise will fade and the plane will slow down. Just how much will depend on you and your size because here we have a tradeoff. If you exit at 130-140 kph (85 mph), the higher speed will provide you with more body control and parachute deployment will be cleaner. However, all this wind makes climbing out and holding on more difficult, so for smaller, weaker students the pilot may throttle back to 115-125 kph.

On the step.

"You swallow hard, thinking to yourself, 'it must be all right, thousands of people have done it before.' Then. . . 'but this time it's me – that's the difference!' " — Charles Shea-Simonds.

"GET ON THE STEP" shouts your jumpmaster with the second exit command. Now you reach across vigorously with the right hand and grasp the strut hooking your fingers around the leading edge. Look forward to the strut and your body and feet will turn toward it. Now pull yourself onto your feet on the step. If you have short arms, you may have to proceed one grip at a time and you'll require some help from your jumpmaster. Poised on the step, keep your weight on your legs; your handholds are for keeping you oriented and balanced. Now that you're set, get your head up and look your jumpmaster in the eye.

Go!

The jumpmaster will emphasize the third and final command "GO!" with a sharp slap across the thigh so you'll know he means you. If you feel anything besides a slap on the thigh, don't jump. You may be past the spot or for some other reason, he may want you to reenter the plane for a go-around. On "GO!", simply step off to the side like you're getting off a bus, then arch your back spreading your arms and legs. Stretch those muscles! Your body will follow your head which is led by the eyes. If you are looking down, you'll probably bend over and do a loop. Look up at your jumpmaster and the result should be a good arch. Pointing your toes also helps. The best body position on exit is perpendicular to the relative wind, about 45 degrees to the ground. If the angle is much more or less than this, a slight rotation may result. At this point in your jump career, your exit position is more important than your body form since you don't have enough airspeed to correct for a poor exit. Make a stable exit. Simultaneous with your exit, you will shout your count beginning with "Arch thousand". This may be practiced at home using a table. The exit and count should be practised until they become smooth and automatic.

As you fall away, your jumpmaster carefully observes your progress and guides your static line.

"On unstable exits, students get a glance at the airplane only about once on each revolution" — Don Grant.

As you fall away, the jumpmaster carefully monitors your body attitude and allows the looped static line to pay out of his hand. He will allow you to fall to the end of the three meter line unless you begin to roll. In this case, he may choke off the S-folds in his hand and ''short line'' you, initiating an earlier deployment, reducing chances of entanglement. He is also making a mental record of your air work which he will discuss with you in the post-jump critique.

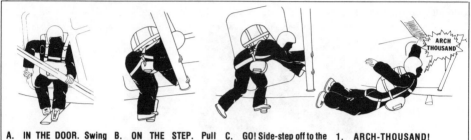

A. IN THE DOOR. Swing legs out into the wind and grasp the wing strut with the left hand. Protect the reserve ripcord handle with the right hand until it is clear of the door.

B. ON THE STEP. Pull yourself out on to the step and face forward grasping the wing strut firmly with both hands. Keep the head up and look at the jumpmaster.

C. GO! Side-step off to the right.

1. ARCH-THOUSAND! Arch your back. Keep the head up and look at the jumpmaster. Start the count sequence out loud:

A capsulized review of the exit.

FRONT

HIGH CENTER OF GRAVITY

(unstable)

BELOW

The spread stable position

LOW CENTER OF GRAVITY

(stable)

You want your canopy to deploy while you are in a stable fall, face to earth, shoulders level position so that it may develop freely, directly away from the body. If your shoulders are level, the skirt of the canopy will not be pulled lower on one side which might cause a partial inversion. A hard arch places your center of gravity low and maintains you in a position like the shuttle cock, face to earth. To learn the principles of stability and to show your friends, use the stability demonstrator described here.

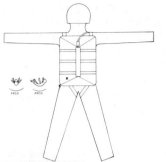

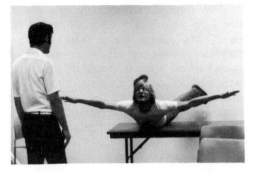

STABILITY DEMONSTRATOR

1. **CUT OUT SKYDIVER** from heavy paper about 22 cm (8.5'') tall by 20 cm (8'') wide.
2. **HOLD IN AIR FACE TO EARTH AND DROP — UNSTABLE**
3. **BEND HEAD, ARMS, AND LEGS UP AND DROP FACE TO EARTH — STABLE**
4. **DROP BACK TO EARTH AND SKYDIVER SLIPS OVER — STABLE**

Stability may be practiced in your livingroom. Lie face down on a table or the floor with the arms and legs extended. Then, on the word "GO!" force a hard arch by lifting the arms, legs and head as high off the floor as possible. See how long you can hold this position. Keep practicing over and over. It will help you to make a better jump and it's great for the stomach muscles.

Once the static line has unlocked the container and pulled out the canopy, you're on your own; your jumpmaster can do nothing now but watch. If you weren't the first student to jump on this lift, you saw him reel in the previous jumper's static line, unhook it and stow it either beneath the pilot's seat or in the rear of the cabin. Meanwhile the pilot was making a 1-2 minute orbit back to jump run for the next student. The jumpmaster is repeating the whole procedure while watching the first student's descent. He may correct the spot if the student misses the target area due to a change in the wind.

Well, so much for all the interesting peripheral discussion, we left you back in freefall, arching and shouting.

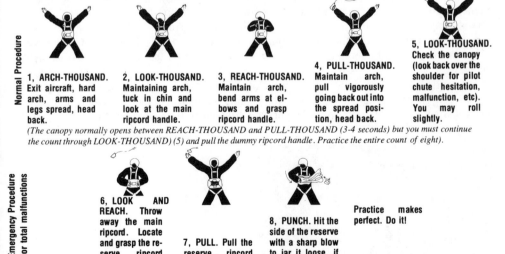

Normal Procedure

1, ARCH-THOUSAND. Exit aircraft, hard arch, arms and legs spread, head back.

2, LOOK-THOUSAND. Maintaining arch, tuck in chin and look at the main ripcord handle.

3, REACH-THOUSAND. Maintain arch, bend arms at elbows and grasp ripcord handle.

4, PULL-THOUSAND. Maintain arch, pull vigorously going back out into the spread position, head back.

5, LOOK-THOUSAND. Check the canopy (look back over the shoulder for pilot chute hesitation, malfunction, etc). You may roll slightly.

(The canopy normally opens between REACH-THOUSAND and PULL-THOUSAND (3-4 seconds) but you must continue the count through LOOK-THOUSAND) (5) and pull the dummy ripcord handle. Practice the entire count of eight).

Emergency Procedure for total malfunctions

6, LOOK AND REACH. Throw away the main ripcord. Locate and grasp the reserve ripcord handle.

7, PULL. Pull the reserve ripcord and throw it away.

8, PUNCH. Hit the side of the reserve with a sharp blow to jar it loose, if necessary.

Practice makes perfect. Do it!

> *"The purpose of the static line jumps is to create a behavior pattern in your mind so that you may safely pull your own ripcord"* — Chuck Ryan.

Many jump operations start their students off making dummy ripcord pulls on the first jump while others teach the spread position initially and then switch to the DRCP motions on jumps two or three. You must continue your count and the indicated movements until the canopy opens bringing you upright. The canopy will normally open between "reach thousand" and "pull thousand" but you must ignore the upward pull and continue the count until you have pulled the dummy ripcord. You won't graduate from the static line to freefall until you not only have five jumps but have demonstrated to your jumpmaster your ability to successfully pull your ripcord on three successive jumps. So, start practicing now.

As you practice your exit count from the table and your arch on the floor, go through the entire count of eight. Practice and practice until it becomes automatic.

As your earthward velocity increases, your hard arch becomes a relaxed, comfortable position.

Total malfunctions are rare but if they didn't occur now and then, we wouldn't bother counting passed "pull thousand". If you reach the count of seven and aren't being jerked upright by your filling canopy, don't hesitate, pull the reserve. It's better to have two canopies out than none. Continue through on the drill and punch the side of the reserve. Occasionally, the grommets hang up momentarily on the cones and require some coaxing to separate.

Of course, there are many other types of malfunctions and remedies but only the "total" normally occurs in this part of the jump sequence. Other parachute malfunctions and some interesting airport dangers are covered in their own chapter.

When in doubt, whip it out. Pull the reserve if you have a total malfunction of the main.

THE OPENING SEQUENCE OF THE SLEEVE DEPLOYED PARACHUTE.

Spread stable position just prior to ripcord pull (or static line activation).

The ripcord is pulled unlocking the container and allowing the spring equipped pilot chute to jump out into the air stream.

Acting like an anchor, the pilot chute draws the sleeved canopy out of the container as the jumper falls away.

The suspension lines unstow from their rubber bands.

As the last two line stows are withdrawn, the sleeve flap is unlocked allowing the sleeve to slide up and off the canopy. The jumper begins to swing upright.

The sleeve is both pulled up by the pilot chute and forced up by the inflating canopy.

The fully exposed canopy begins to inflate from the apex downward. The jumper is nearly upright.

After a brief rebounding inversion, the canopy is fully inflated and stabilizes in a steady descent. The sleeve and pilot chute, attached by the sleeve retainer line, fall down and rest on top.

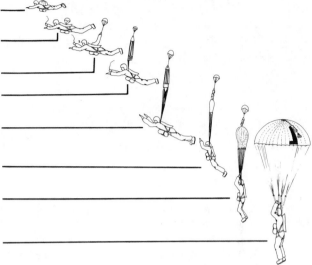

But you are pulled upright by your blossoming canopy and you experience an overwhelming exhilaration. You look up to see your new nylon friend, the one who plucked you from freefall, and find the canopy to be larger than you imagined. You're at 800 meters (2,600′) and it's beautiful! The air is brisk and clean. It's so quiet! You can hear people talking on the ground over a half mile away. But this is no time for sightseeing; time's a wasting and there is work to be done.

CANOPY CONTROL. Wind determination and steering the canopy. A 2½ to 3 minute ride.
AFTER OPENING.
A. LOOK UP. Check the canopy*. Disconnect automatic opener. Stow the ripcord handle. Grasp the steering toggles.
B. LOOK DOWN. Get oriented: find the target and the wind sock. Determine the wind line. To turn right, pull down on the right toggle; to turn left, pull down on the left toggle (to stop the turn, let the toggle back up). Listen or watch for ground instructions.

* Partial malfunctions are covered in the emergency procedures chapter.

Your canopy ride has three distinct phases. The canopy check, steering for the target and preparing to land. Look up and check the canopy. If it is anything but perfect, you will follow the instructions as outlined in the chapter on emergency procedures. Now disconnect your automatic opener if you are using one. Stow your dummy ripcord handle. You may slip it under a pack opening band on the reserve or slip it down the front of your jumpsuit. Don't lose it! Dropped from half a mile up it could injure someone on the ground and, besides, most clubs have penalties for lost ripcords, usually beginning with a case of beer. Now reach up and grasp the steering lines by their wooden toggles on the rear risers.

Look down at the ground and get yourself oriented. Find the target and head for it. Listen or watch for ground instructions as you have been taught. Your DZ may be using radios, a bull horn, P.A. system, ground panels, etc. to guide you down.

The small end of the windsock points in the direction the wind is going.

Find the windsock. It will not only show you the direction of the wind, with practice you will be able to judge wind speed by its angle. Later you will use other wind indicators such as smoke from factory chimneys, ripples on ponds, flags, etc. Winds vary in direction and intensity at different levels and this will become more important when you reach long freefalls.

Your ride from opening to landing will be influenced by four major factors: gravity, wind (speed and direction), canopy forward speed and other atmospheric conditions. While you can't expect to make precision landings right from the start, an understanding of certain basics will enable you to avoid obstacles by steering around them.

SPEED CONVERSION TABLE		
METERS PER SEC	M.P.H.	LIMITATIONS
1	2.25	
2	4.5	
3	6.75	Upper limit for students:
4	9	4.5 mps or 10mph
5	11.25	
6	13.5	
7	15.75	Most experienced
8	18	jumpers stop at 9 mps,
9	20	about 20 mph.

Gravity, the first factor affecting your flight, depends on the total weight of you and all your parachute gear. If you weigh 73 kg (160 lbs.) and have 18 kg (40 lbs.) of gear including parachutes, boots, helmet, etc, you can expect to descend at about 5mps (1,000 fpm) under a standard 28' canopy with a Double L steering vent modification. This means you'll have about two and a half minutes from the time you open at 750m until you touch down. If you weigh more, you'll come down faster. In fact, if you weigh much more, you'll be issued a larger canopy and then you'll have to start all these calculations over.

"The quiet amazes me. With the chute doing its job, the ride down is a piece of cake"

PARACHUTE STEERABILITY

TURNING the CANOPY
pull the toggle
all the way down

FORWARD SPEED
4 mps (9 mph)
in still air.

As it descends, your canopy scoops air and drags it along. It is a big scoop, moving right along and the quantity of air captured is a lot. The air must escape and it does. Some goes through the 18'' vent in the apex and much passes through the porous fabric itself. What is left 'spills' out from under the lower lateral band or skirt and this random spilling sets up a pendulum-like swinging motion in the load (you) called ''oscillations''. But your government surplus canopy has been ''modified'' for steerability and forward speed, probably with a Double L vent configuration. Now if you weigh 73 kg you can expect a canopy speed of almost 15 km/h and a glide angle of 38 degrees. The air escaping to the rear is pushing the canopy forward just like a rear-engined Volkswagen.

Which way is the wind blowing? Are you drifting
toward or away from the target?

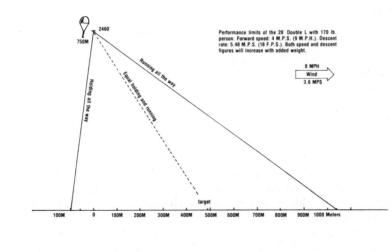

Performance limits of the 28' Double L with 170 lb. person. Forward speed: 4 M.P.S. (9 M.P.H.). Descent rate: 5.48 M.P.S. (18 F.P.S.). Both speed and descent figures will increase with added weight.

You at 15 kph ⟶ ⟵ wind at 10 kph = a ground speed of 5 kph.
You at 15 kph ⟶ ⟶ wind at 10 kph = a ground speed of 25 kph.

The canopy is designed to run at its maximum forward speed when the steering toggles are all the way up.

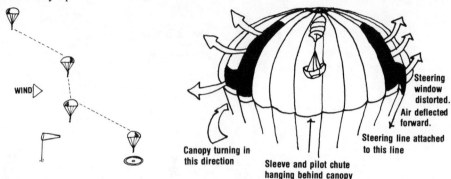

WIND▷

Steering window distorted.
Air deflected forward.

Steering line attached to this line

Canopy turning in this direction

Sleeve and pilot chute hanging behind canopy

The turning of the canopy is accomplished by pulling down on the steering line on the side to which you wish to turn. The faster and further you pull the line down, the quicker the canopy will turn. Fast turns also make you swing out from under the canopy in a wide arc and increase the rate of descent somewhat. Because of this swinging and increased descent rate, major turns should not be made near the ground. It is best to make all turns gently. Toggles should be pulled down in front of you where you can see your hands in relation to the turn being produced.

Pulling down on both toggles evenly will cause the canopy to "brake" or slow its forward speed. Some canopy modifications brake better than others. The "T" is poor and the "TU" is good. Braking also increases the rate of descent so you won't be experimenting with it for a while. This is covered in greater detail in the equipment chapter.

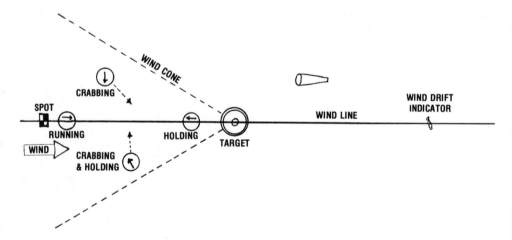

Did you open over the opening point? If you are upwind (deep), you will be "running" with the wind a lot, while if you opened closer to the target than you planned, you will spend most of your canopy ride "holding" against the wind. If you find yourself left or right of the opening point, you are off the "wind line" and will be "crabbing" across the wind to get back to it. If the opening point was correct and if you opened over it, you will require an equal amount of running and holding to hit the target. You will use extra running and holding only to compensate for changes in the wind speed. You will use crabbing to make up for wind direction changes. Since holding provides you the slowest drift across the ground, you should make your landings into the wind.

After opening, turn and face the target. If you are on the wind line, the target will appear to be moving toward you, remaining stationary or moving away from you. If it is moving toward you, turn and hold so as not to overshoot it. While holding, make slight turns so you can watch the target and its movement while you are holding. If it moves away from you, turn and run toward it. If the target appears to be moving to one side, you're off the wind line and must crab back to it.

The wind line is drawn in the direction of the wind and runs through the opening point and the center of the target. It shifts as the wind and opening point shift. You may venture off the wind line and still make it to the target as long as you remain in the "wind cone". Initially, you'll probably experience some difficulty in relating your altitude, air time and the capabilities of your canopy. This is not crucial on your first jump and your skill and understanding will improve with experience.

The wind cone is that maneuvering area to either side of the wind line which will still allow you to land on the target. The "cone" becomes narrower as the wind increases.

WIND

Wind Line
Opening Point
TARGET
Limit of Maneuver for 'Double L' Canopy
Limit of Maneuver for High Performance Canopy

The "Wind Cone"

CANOPY RANGE
OPENING POINT
CANOPY RANGE
CANOPY RANGE
TARGET

Three dimensional diagram showing wind cone under no wind condition. (Cone is vertical).

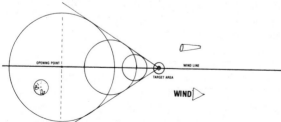

OPENING POINT
WIND LINE
TARGET AREA
WIND

The wind cone with wind added. As long as you descend within this cone, you will have the ability to get back on the wind line and hit the target.

If the good Lord had wanted man to stay on the ground, he would have given us roots.

The closer you get to the target, both horizontally and vertically, the less room you have to maneuver laterally. Note that the wind cone becomes smaller as you descend. If you stay within it, you will have the ability to return to the wind line and hit the target. But if, for example, you venture just 5 meters outside it, there is no way you can land any closer than 5 meters from the target. When you are in the center of the cone, all headings are equally correct. But as you move nearer to the side of the cone your options of best choices decrease and when you reach the edge of the cone, your directional choices are reduced to one.

The three examples below show the correct path of your canopy for the following three situations:

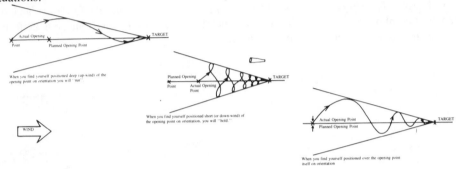

The principle is simply that if you are deep, you must use the wind to assist you to cover more ground and if you are short, you must counteract the wind by holding. The ideal spot will permit you to make gentle S-turns astride the wind line. If the target begins to move closer or farther away, you will adjust the concentration of your S-turns accordingly.

There are also certain atmospheric conditions which will affect your spotting and canopy ride. At higher elevations such as Denver, your descent rate will be faster since the air is rarer. Similarly, descent rates increase when the barometric pressure drops or when the air is humid and/or on hot days.

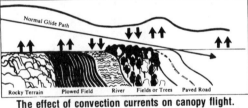

The effect of convection currents on canopy flight.

Changes on a single jump may be felt as you cross certain areas such as a forest to a highway. Some areas absorb and give off more of the sun's heat than others. Some areas such as runways, tin roofs, etc. may produce thermals, boiling bubbles of warmed air which rise quickly. If you pass through one of these invisible lift machines, you will ascend a bit and your canopy ride may be extended by several minutes.

SPEED CONVERSION TABLE			
METERS PER SECOND	MPH	KM per hour	Knots
0.45	1	1.609	0.87
0.89	2	3.219	1.74
1.34	3	4.828	2.61
1.78	4	6.437	3.47
2.23	5	8.046	4.34
2.68	6	9.656	5.21
3.12	7	11.265	6.88
3.57	8	12.874	6.95
4.02	9	14.484	7.82
4.47	10	16.093	8.68
For higher speeds, add the applicable figures.			

You are about to enter the third and final phase of the canopy ride, the preparation for the parachute landing fall, or "PLF". In steering your canopy at this point, you want to concentrate on two areas. First, you want your canopy headed directly into the wind to minimize your ground speed, your horizontal movement over the ground. So you'll face the opening point upwind of the target and check the wind sock to see if there have been any minor changes in the lower ground winds. Secondly, during the last 75m and 15 seconds, you want to avoid all but very minor corrective turns to the canopy since a large turn will only increase your horizontal travel by swinging you out from under the canopy. And, let's not forget that canopy descent increases during turns. So let's land with a stable canopy, landing as slowly as possible. Now here you are at 75m, positioned over the drop zone in the vicinity of the target and preparing to land. Caution. Feeling wind in your face doesn't indicate you're "faced into the wind". You will always feel wind in your face because the canopy is moving forward through the air. Look at the ground to gauge your horizontal drift.

A "PLF" is a method of falling down on landing which translates the vertical energy, which can smart, into a rotational energy, which won't, without placing any breakable bony part of your body on the ground until the process is successfully completed. There is a lot of energy which must be absorbed, so spread it around while protecting the areas subject to breaking. A correctly executed PLF will not only make jumping more comfortable and enjoyable when landing on the DZ, a prepared landing area, it may save you from serious injury if you're blown out of the target area and must land on hard or uneven surfaces.

Some landings can be potentially extremely hazardous such as when descending into water, power lines or trees. If any of these dangers occur in the area of your DZ, your instructor will make special reference to them and will outline a particular corrective action. We will cover them and others in detail in the chapter on emergency procedures.

CANOPY DESCENT		equal to jumping from a table this high:	
MPS	FPS		
9	30	13'	4M
		12'	
8		10'	3M
	25	9'	
7		8'	
		7'	
6	20	6'	2M
		5'	
5	15	4'	
		3'	1M
4		2'	
3	10	1'	

NOTE RELATIONSHIPS

You can expect a landing shock equal to jumping from a 4' table. But there is some horizontal movement so it is more like jumping off the trunk of a car doing 3 mph. For more details on descent rates, see the equipment chapter.

A. PREPARE TO LAND (at about 200' over clear ground)
Face into the wind to minimize horizontal drift. Hands on steering toggles making slight corrections.

WIND & FALL LINE

Feet and knees together, knees bent slightly, toes extended downward and look down at 45°. Grab back risers & pull down. Elbows in.

B. GROUND CONTACT. *Toes.* Leg muscles tensed and prepared to absorb ninety percent of the impact force.

Rotate body in the direction of the fall allowing the knees to move in the direction of force. Head down.

Calf. Elbows and hands forward in front of chest and face.

Thigh. Keep the elbows in.

C. FOLLOW THROUGH Stand up and run around the canopy to dump its air and deflate it. If you are being dragged and cannot get up, roll over on your back and pull down all the way on one toggle or jettison the canopy.

Butt. Continue roll in one long smooth continuous motion.

Shoulder. First one . . .

and then on through to the other.

Feet. Over, contacting with the line of fall (wind line) so that the canopy will aid in pulling you to your feet.

This is a forward-left P.L.F., the most common. Your drift may dictate that it be to the back or to the side but the principle is the same: to distribute the landing force over as much of the body as possible.

One second is about all it takes to make the PLF, not much time to think about or change your landing plans. Even though you have set up for the PLF faced into the wind to minimize ground speed, there will probably be some horizontal drift. Actually, PLFs are easier with some drift than when coming straight down. On contact, you will execute your PLF in the direction of drift and it may be in any direction, forward, backward, to one side or the other. You will practice landings from a low platform but it might be more accurate to leap from the trunk of a car going some 3 mph.

Think about the PLF in three parts: the vertical force absorption, the horizontal force absorption and getting back on your feet. Prepare to land: just prior to touchdown, your toes are bent down, your knees are slightly bent (unlocked) and your leg muscles are tensed to absorb perhaps 90 percent of the vertical force, your feet and knees are pressed firmly together so that you'll be able to roll. You're looking down at 45 degrees, not away from the ground and not directly at it. At this angle, you can better judge your altitude. Your hands are on the toggles so now you bring your elbows almost together in front of your face, grasp the rear risers and pull down as though you were beginning to chin yourself. Tuck your head forward and down to avoid whiplash in the case of a backward landing. Watch the ground at 45 degrees in order to anticipate it and begin your roll, noting the direction of drift so that you will roll with it.

In the old days, instructors told students to look at the horizon and commence the roll when they felt their feet touch the ground. But after some study, it has been found that you are descending too fast to execute a roll once the ground is sensed. After a few jumps and a couple of bruises, you'll be looking down anyway so you might as well begin on your first jump. Your knees are bent but tensioned to accept the vertical force. You are protecting your breakable elbows by bringing them together in front of you and "hanging" on the risers. As soon as you touch down and take the tension out of the canopy system, this hanging will automatically force your head and elbows down and into a protected position while rounding your shoulders to better accept the roll. It will also tend to shift you forward in the saddle placing your feet down and under you where they belong.

You touch the ground absorbing most of the shock in your leg muscles. Limp leg muscles are probably the foremost cause of injuries on landing. If you have good leg muscle tension with your legs firmly together and knees unlocked, you are unlikely to be hurt on landing. Practice and discipline yourself! If your legs are limp, you'll wind up with a bruised hip and will find walking difficult until just before it's time to return next weekend for your next jump. You may even manage to remain standing if there is little horizontal drift but it isn't likely with your feet and knees pressed tightly together. Even if you feel you can remain on your feet, it is a good idea to continue through with the PLF both for the practice and because the DZ Safety Officer will give you a good chewing out if you don't.

There is some drift today so it's time to take care of it. As you are absorbing the vertical force, shift the pressed knees and rotate your shoulders and trunk toward the fall line. Keep the elbows, hands and head in, let yourself go. You'll roll like a ball. Continue on through and spring back up on your feet. Try practicing the vertical and horizontal parts of the landing separately and then use a platform to go through the whole PLF. Jump, absorb forces in the legs, roll and stand up.

There is a lot to remember and it will be difficult to select and execute the proper PLF for each line of drift; which way to shift and rotate. You'll also find that PLFs use new muscles so don't be surprised if you have trouble getting out of bed tomorrow.

Knowing some of the common mistakes may help you to avoid them. Some students anticipate the ground and begin their landing roll before they reach it; the vertical forces are not absorbed by the legs. Some put their legs out in front of them and some go entirely limp. All three produce bruises and occasionally a break. Backing up landings sometimes result in a feet-butt-head ground contact which is to be avoided. If you find yourself backing up in strong winds, turn the canopy as much as 45 degrees from the wind line so you'll be able to make a PLF. Similarly, if the wind is very light and you are moving forward, you'll want to turn slightly again. This will permit you to do a PLF rather than a FHF (feet, hands, face). Some canopies have slight built in turns and all canopies suffer occasionally from turns when the sleeve and pilot chute hang up in a slot. You may wish to keep the toggles in your hands. If your knees are not firmly pressed together, you will tend to sit down on touchdown absorbing the force in the wrong area. That may be your last sitting for a while.

You will probably be guided by ground signals, radio, bull horn or panels. But equipment fails, DZ personnel may be off helping the student ahead of you and, of course, it always helps to understand what you are doing.

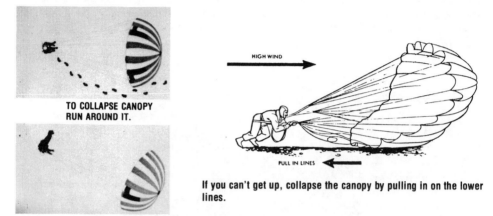

TO COLLAPSE CANOPY RUN AROUND IT.

If you can't get up, collapse the canopy by pulling in on the lower lines.

After you land, get up on your feet immediately and run around your canopy to spill the air out of it.

Your PLF should lead into an immediate recovery in order to avoid being dragged by the wind or covered by the deflating canopy. Once you touch down, your next project is to collapse the canopy. Of course, if you happen to have a no-wind day, the canopy will deflate without your assistance but it may fall all around you in a tangled mess. If you're quick in following through on your PLF and get up on your feet, you will be able to run out from under it keeping the lines tensioned and straight. But there is usually some wind and during your student career, it should be light. And you'll want to get right back up on your feet for another reason: you want to show the DZ Safety Officer that you are OK. Some students are so overcome by their recent accomplishment that they just want to lie on the ground, relax and think about it. That is one sure way to draw an immediate well intentioned crowd.

There are five basic ways to spill the air from an inflated canopy. 1, Get up and run around either side of it to turn the canopy out of the wind. 2, have a buddy grab the apex or skirt and pull the canopy around. 3, in light winds, you can pull down all the way on a steering line to rotate the canopy driving it into the ground and letting the air escape from the holes in the back. 4, grab the riser and then the lines closest to the ground and pull them toward you hand over hand. And 5, jettison the canopy by activating the shoulder mounted canopy releases. Number five is a last ditch method and it is doubtful that you will experience winds strong enough to need it. If you are equipped with a Stevens Cutaway System, you'll have to disconnect it first and then activate both riser releases because the risers are connected with a cross strap. Jettisoning a riser will make a tangled mess of the canopy and in high winds, it will take off like shot from a sling so don't attempt it on a crowded DZ.

If you are being dragged, guard the reserve. It is easy to drag out the ripcord handle. Repairing a damaged reserve canopy can be very expensive so let the container take the abuse. The most important thing to remember in your recovery is to act quickly. A gentle dragging across the DZ can begin as an entertaining ride and quickly transform into a high speed, dangerous situation where you are not in complete control.

Other jumpers will probably come over, pump your hand and welcome you to the great world-wide fraternity of parachuting. They know your excitement and both want to encourage it and join you in your moment of glory. If you are in the target area, you should pull the canopy off to one side to uncover the disc for the next jumper.

Now comes the field care of your parachute or preparing it for transport back to the packing area. The normal method is to "field pack" the parachute. Take off your reserve and shed the harness. Pull the canopy out straight and pull the sleeve over the canopy while someone holds onto the sleeve retainer line and then the canopy apex. Then chain link the suspension lines and accordion fold all of this back and forth in the container. Pull the flaps up and lock with the pack opening bands. With the direct bag system, stretch out the canopy, chain link the lines and then accordion fold the canopy itself back and forth in the container.

The field packed main parachute. Just sling it naturally over both shoulders, fasten the chest strap and snap on the reserve for balance.

Chain link the lines and loop them over your neck.

Figure eight the canopy around the arms.

Lay the pilot chute and deployment device on top.

"You know it is Spring when the four feet of snow which covered the runway making it impossible to jump, have melted to one foot of mud, making it impossible to jump" — The Spotter Newsmagazine.

If you are very close to the packing area and plan to make another jump with that same parachute very soon, you may wish to pick up your canopy like the big boys. Just stretch out your arms and figure eight the lines and canopy around them.

It is time for your jump debriefing or after-jump critique from your jumpmaster who has only recently arrived on the target. If you are to learn from your experience and improve upon it, you must solicit an objective observation of your performance. He'll check with the DZ safety officer on your canopy work and he may debrief all the students at one time. This is to your advantage as you will learn from the experiences of others. First, he will probably ask you what you did. This helps you to remember and he wants to know what you think, how you interpret your performance. Then he'll tell you what he and the DZ Safety Officer saw so you can re-evaluate your impressions with this (new) information. He will prescribe some corrective ground practice and will tell you what to concentrate on during the next jump.

The jump will be recorded in your log book, criticisms and all, in order to maintain a continuing record of your parachuting progress. This is for your reference, his benefit and for any other jumpmasters you may have on future jumps. This log will be with you forever so learn how to fill it out before you take pen in hand and keep it neat.

If you are jumping with a club, you'll probably venture to the packing area next to repack your parachute. If this is a commercial center, they'll do it for you and you are free to sign up for jump number two. Many, many students make two jumps the first day. Incidentally, Richard Bach, the author of Jonathan Livingston Seagull, made seven jumps, including two freefalls, his first day out. But jumping, especially all the preparation, is tiring and you will probably be limited to three jumps per day initially. If you hustle, you can be on freefall by next weekend!

You've done it. It's been a long day and you've accomplished and learned so much. You have a greater appreciation for the air, aviation, weather and especially yourself. You notice the wind, its direction and velocity. Weather no longer provides ''nice days'' and ''lousy days'', now they are ''jumpable'' or terrible. You begin to look up and you notice many things you have never seen before. Canopy nylon has a great smell all its own. And you have a warm feeling of new-found confidence. Anyone can jump but few people will. You did it and you're proud. You have conquered another fear, that of falling. It's just like when you learned to swim, only better.

Your instruction does not end with your first jump. You will be carefully supervised until you acquire your first license. Then the challenges change but the learning continues as you work on your parachuting proficiency. Always remember to ask your instructor about any area which is not clear to you.

CHAPTER III
PARACHUTING DOWN THROUGH THE AGES,
A Brief History

During the last ten centuries, parachutes and parachuting have passed through three basic developmental stages. The earliest occurred before the balloon and other aircraft; before there was an actual need. The second was during the last three centuries when there was a requirement to be able to escape damaged balloons, airplanes and spacecraft. And the last stage is taking place from the 1950's to the present within the sport of parachuting. The sport requires significantly different equipment and it is probably true that during the last 15 years there have been more improvements to the parachute than in all of previous recorded history.

1100's. There is evidence the Chinese amused themselves by jumping from high places with rigid umbrella-like structures. Early accounts are impossible to verify due to the lack of recorded data and it should be noted that most parachutes were one of a kind; there was no standardization until World War I. Further, after careful study, one suspects that many of these early pioneers confused vertical descent with horizontal flight. They probably wished to emulate the birds not the down of a thistle.

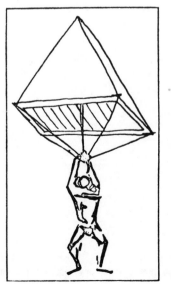

da Vinci's parachute

1495. Leonardo da Vinci's parachute was pyramid shaped and was held open by four wooden poles. There is no evidence that he constructed any working models; he left only a sketch.

Veranzio's parachute

1595. Fausto Veranzio's parachute consisted of a square wooden frame covered with canvas and it is claimed he jumped from a tower in Venice in either 1595 or 1617.

1687. One of the earliest written accounts of parachuting comes from Siam. According to the French envoy, one of the king's tumblers would jump from high places with two large umbrellas. The launch point must have been quite high as the wind sometimes carried him into trees, roof tops and occasionally the river.

Lenormand jumps from a rooftop in Montpelier, France.

42

1783. Sebastian Lenormand jumped from a tower with a 14 foot diameter parachute hoping to perfect a way to escape burning buildings. The Montgolfier brothers, famous balloonists, tested various parachute designs. In one experiment, a sheep was safely lowered on a 7 foot canopy.

1785. J.P. Blanchard devised the collapsible silk parachute. Prior to this all canopies had been held open by a rigid framework. There is some evidence that he jumped from a balloon in 1793 and he did break a leg about this time.

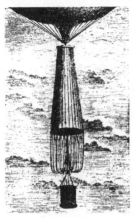

Garnerin descends over London in 1802.

1797. André Jacques Garnerin gets credit for being the first real parachutist because he made so many jumps beginning with one from 600M (2000 feet) over Paris. In 1802, he made a jump from 8000 feet over London with a silk canopy some 23 feet in diameter. It oscillated terribly making him airsick.

1804. A Frenchman named Bourget jumped with a collapsible canopy. Lelandes, a French astronomer, added a vent to his canopy to reduce the oscillations and it worked.

1808. A Polish balloonist named Jodaki Kuparento made the first emergency jump when his balloon caught fire over Warsaw.

Early 1800's. Sir George Cayley, an English aviation pioneer, was the first to propose an inverted cone canopy. Lorenz Hengler, a German, made several jumps from a balloon at 30 to 120 meters. It was very unstable. This design is being investigated again today.

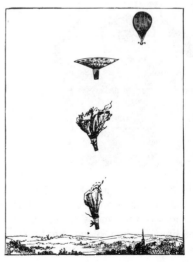

Robert Cocking, the first parachuting fatality

43

1837. Robert Cocking released his inverted cone parachute over Lea Green in England and fell to his death when it collapsed. It was 107 feet in circumference and weighed over 200 lbs. The release was on the balloon not the canopy and it is supposed that he may have wrapped the release line around his wrist to obtain a better grip. This would have jerked him upward into the cone, breaking it.

1838. John Wise twice permitted his balloon to explode at 13,000 feet over the U.S. Each time the underside of the envelope inverted assuming a parachute shape and lowering him safely.

1887. Captain Tom Baldwin invented the harness in the U.S. He would ride the balloon up sitting on a trapeze bar. The apex of the silk canopy was tied to the trapeze. When ready to jump, he would simply slip off. He dispensed with the basket entirely.

Käthe Paulus was the first German professional parachutist. The "folded exhibition attached type" was used by many of the early jumpers. Here the suspension lines were attached to a concentration ring made of wood with a tennis racket like mesh. The lines were coiled on the mesh and the canopy was accordian folded on the lines. Two perpendicular tie ropes secured the canopy to the ring. A ring knife was used to release the canopy and there was a breakcord from the apex of the canopy to the balloon.

Mike Blodgett models a variation of the pack on the aircraft type parachute. The container is fitted with a Ford steering wheel and is laced together with string. Two thin leather leg straps are missing from the model. Newspaper is packed between the folds of canopy and loops of line.

1890. Paul Letteman and Käthe Paulus are credited with being the first to use the "remote automatic attached sack type" parachute; the design is still used for cargo drops today. The apex of the canopy is tied to the inside of the canvas bag with breakcord. The canopy and lines are then folded in to the bag and the mouth is tied closed with breakcord. The risers lead out to the load and the bag is affixed to the balloon, airplane, etc.

The Broadwick Coatpack

1901. Charles Broadwick designed the "pack on the aviator" type parachute. His "coat pack" was laced together with breakcord. A static line broke the lacing and pulled out the canopy.

1903. The Wright brothers made the first powered flight and parachute development picked up speed.

1908. A. Leo Stevens invents the ripcord in New York. Georgia Thompson (Tiny) Broadwick begins her 1,100 jump career by parachuting from a balloon over Raleigh, North Carolina. She used the parachutes designed by her foster father Charles Broadwick.

1911. An Italian named Joseph Pino gets credit for designing the pilot chute. He mounted it on an aviators' cap. It was held open by a small framework. When he jumped, the pilot chute was supposed to remove the helmet and pull the canopy from the "knapsack" on his back. Grant Morton didn't use any pack at all when he jumped from a Wright Model B aircraft over Venice, California. He simply rolled and folded the canopy in his arms. When he jumped, he just threw it into the air. While this was the first non-static line jump, it may not be the first freefall jump; there is a question of interpretation. S.L. Van Meter of Lexington, Kentucky, filed for a patent on a "soaring type parachute". A pilot in distress could pull a ripcord releasing the canopy into the air and it would pull him free of the aircraft. G.E. Kotelnikov had his parachute designs rejected by the Russian government; they felt that the presence of a parachute would tempt pilots to jump rather than attempt to save the aircraft.

1912. When Captain Albert Berry made his jump from an aircraft over Jefferson Barracks, Missouri, his parachute was packed in a metal cylinder attached to the underside of the plane over the axle. He just climbed down to the axle, slipped into the harness and jumped. As he fell away, his weight pulled the canopy from the container. About this same time, M. Hervieu was making dummy drops from the Eiffel Tower. M. Bonnet successfully lowered an airplane fuselage with a dummy from a balloon over France.

"The gull sees farthest who flies highest" – Richard Bach

1913. M. Adolphe Pegoud successfully tested a soaring type parachute over Chateaufort, France. Captain M. Douade designed a canopy for lowering entire aircraft but World War I cancelled his development plans.

Tiny Broadwick is credited with many parachuting firsts.

Tiny Broadwick became the first woman to jump from an airplane when Glenn Martin took her aloft over Los Angeles. Later that year she became the first woman to make a water jump when she parachuted from a hydroplane into Lake Michigan.

1914. Tiny Broadwick was demonstrating the parachute to the Army in San Diego when on her fourth jump, the static line caught briefly on the tail section of the Martin Trainer. Fearful it might happen again, she cut the line. On the last demonstration jump, she pulled it herself and made history: the first jump on a manually operated parachute.

1915. A British experimenter, Col. H.S. Holt first became interested in parachutes as a means for lowering flares. Many of his designs had both pilot chutes and drogues. He advocated the use of drogue chutes for stability to enable the flier to freefall to lower altitudes to avoid enemy fire. He would release the drogue into the airstream, jump after it, freefall, reel in the drogue and pull the ripcord. Col. Maitland, a British experimenter jumped from a reported altitude of 10,000 feet with a parachute of his own design. Also in this year, the German Balloon Parachute was placed in service. Based on the design of Miss Paulus, it had a line to the apex for altering the rate of descent.

1917. Most nations adopted parachutes for use in balloons (there was no time to evaluate the situation once the hydrogen filled balloon was hit by enemy fire) and airplanes as the aerial portion of World War I heated up. All operated on the static line principle, were too heavy and much too weak. Juseke Fuji of Stanton, New Mexico, filed a patent on a manually operated parachute. And late in the year, J. Floyd Smith wore a manually operated parachute of his own design while flying.

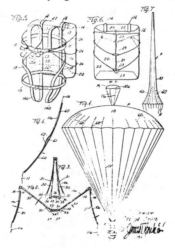

The original Smith patent on the manually operated parachute

1918. Floyd Smith filed for a patent on his manually operated parachute.

1919. Leslie Irvin developed a static line operated parachute and filed for a patent.

The Smith Aerial Life Pack was the first of the modern manually operated parachutes.

The Army set up a parachute design center at McCook Field in Dayton and staffed it with Floyd Smith and Major E.L. Hoffman. On April 28th, Leslie Irvin made a freefall jump to test the product as Floyd Smith piloted the plane. The manually operated parachute was basically the same one that Smith had designed earlier. Irvin immediately formed "Irving Air Chutes" and built the first 300 units for the Army. A rushed typist mistakenly added the "g" to Irvin and the company kept it for some fifty years. The McCook Field team consisted of Hoffman, Smith, Irvin, Guy M. Ball, "Jimmy" M. Russell, J.J. Higgins, and Sgt. Ralph W. Bottreil. Most remained in the parachute field and were responsible for virtually all of the parachute development over the next 30 years.

1922. Lt. Harold R. Harris became the first to make an emergency freefall jump from a disabled airplane. He had difficulty locating the ripcord handle and freefell some 2,000 feet. It is interesting to contrast this jump with all those made in World War I; they were all static lined. One month later, the Caterpillar Club was established. Those who were saved by parachute were awarded a small gold (silk spinning) caterpillar pin.

1924. The parachute rigging school was opened at the Naval Air Station at Lakehurst, New Jersey.

1925. Steven Budreau, an Army instructor made a jump from 7,000 feet and freefell to 3,500 feet over Selfridge Field, Michigan. He proved that the body could fall in a stable position and not go out of control.

1926. Charles Lindbergh makes his fourth emergency jump. Later that same year, James Clark made the first camera jump.

Colonel Charles A. Lindbergh buckling on his Parachute Harness

(Inset) Lindbergh as a graduate flying cadet.

From the infield of the racetrack of the fair grounds at Rochester, N.H., Charles Dame goes aloft for a triple parachute jump. The three parachute packs are visible just above his head. (September 1927)

1927. Charles Lindbergh made the first transatlantic solo flight. This was also the year that Security Parachute Co. was established as Johnny's Parachute Loft at the Oakland Airport and the Switlik Company began making parachutes in Trenton, New Jersey.

1928. General Billy Mitchell had six military men jump from a Martin bomber at Kelly Field, Texas, and set up a machine gun. This was the first demonstration of the usefulness of paratroops.

1929. E.L. Hoffman filed for a patent on his triangular shaped canopy. The quick release box was patented in Great Britain thus making a single point release harness possible.

1930. The Russians stage the first parachute meet at the Sports Festival. Amateurs competed to see who could land nearest a specified target.

1932. 40 parachutists competed at the National Air Races at Roosevelt Field, New York. The organizational work is credited to Joe Crane who persuaded the National Aeronautic Association to formally sanction sport parachuting competitions. Later he formed the National Parachute Jumpers Association, a predecessor of the USPA.

1933. The Russians unified all sport parachute clubs into a national organization. Later they staged the first mass drop when 62 parachutists jumped from three bombers. This was also the year Wiley Post made the first solo flight around the world.

1934. Floyd Smith published a magazine article describing freefall techniques for delayed jumps. The Forest Service experimented with the dropping of fire fighters to battle forest fires. Later, the "Smoke Jumpers" were established.

1935. The first free-drop parachute tower, some 125 feet high, was built in Hightstown, New Jersey. And, this was the year that the infamous DC-3 made its first flight.

1936. By this time, the Russians had established 559 training towers and 115 training stations. In the U.S. during the late 30's, there were some steerable canopies such as the Hoffman Triangle and the Hart designs. But designers turned back to the non-steerable models in the 40's.

1937. The first flight of the Twin Beech. This aircraft was to become used extensively for parachuting in the 1960's and lead to the formation of ten man teams; the number of parachutists it would hold.

1938. Floyd Smith and Lyman Ford approach Henry R. Mallory at the 100 year old Cheney Brothers Mills in Manchester, Connecticut, proposing to form a parachute company. Pioneer Parachute Co. was established and Smith designed a completely new line of parachutes. World War II was not far off.

1941. The Germans dropped 14,000 paratroops onto the island of Crete. In the U.S., Arthur H. Starnes made a record freefall from 30,800 feet to 1,500 feet. Carefully monitored by doctors, he proved that properly equipped aviators could survive long delays from high altitudes.

1944. Frank Derry applied his "Derry Slots" to some 28' military reject canopies to bolster the dwindling Forest Service inventory. This was a significant action as he was modifying surplus canopies for steerability for the first time.

1946. The National Parachute Jumpers Association changed its name to the National Parachute Jumpers-Riggers, Inc.

1947. Charles E. Yeager made the first supersonic flight over the United States. More improvements in the parachute would be needed.

1948. On the prompting of Joe Crane, the NAA proposed to the Fédération Aéronautique Internationale, the international body which governs sport aviation competition and records, that parachuting be accepted. The Commission Internationale de Parachutisme was established and Crane was appointed the first U.S. delegate. Leo "Birdman" Valentin developed the spread face to earth freefall position and later the method of using the arms and legs to make controlled turns and barrel rolls. He was killed in 1956 while using large plywood wings to extend his freefall time. One hit the plane on exit and broke placing him in a spin. He activated both parachutes but they tangled around him.

1949. The French government set up ten public sport parachuting centers. The techniques of stablized freefall were further refined.

1950. Captain Richard V. Wheeler bails out at a record 42,449 feet.

1951. Five European nations fielded teams to the First World Parachuting Championships in Yugoslavia.

1952. Lew Sanborn issued license A-1, A.R. Garrison issued B-1 and Joe Crane issued C-1.

1954. Fred Mason, an Army Sergeant stationed in Europe, represented the U.S. at the Second World Parachuting Championships at St. Yan, France. Eight nations were represented. Richard Hart filed a patent on an extended "T" cut in standard flat circular canopies.

1955. Jacques André Istel visited France, learned the freefall techniques and returned home to form the first U.S. parachute team.

1956. The first U.S. Team was fielded for the Third World Championships in Moscow using borrowed equipment. They finished sixth out of the ten nations entered.

1957. The NPJ-R evolved into the Parachute Club of America. Jacques Istel and Lew Sanborn filed for a patent on the deployment sleeve.

1958. Lyle Hoffman and James Pearson of the Seattle Skydivers made the first baton pass in Vancouver, B.C. A month later, Steve Snyder and Charlie Hillard made the first in the U.S. at Fort Bragg, North Carolina. This was the year that the Army reversed its stand against sport parachuting and actually began to foster and encourage it. Military parachute clubs blossomed nation wide overnight. The U.S. Team was picked at an elimination meet for the first time and the winners went on to compete at the Fourth W.P.C. in Bratislava, Czechoslovakia. The U.S. finished sixth out of 14. Jacques Istel files for a patent on the "three panel T" and "double blank" steerable modifications.

Steve Snyder and Charlie Hillard

1959. Lew Sanborn issued license D-1. The Strategic Army Corps Parachute Team was formed in Fort Bragg. Two years later they were renamed the Army Parachute Team and soon after they adopted the nickname "Golden Knights". Dave Burt developed the para-scuba concept. Jacques Istel's Parachutes Incorporated opened the first commercial sport parachuting center in the U.S. in Orange, Massachusetts. In the late 50's, the sport of parachuting began to grow and equipment played a large part in this development. The sleeve, introduced from France, made opening forces tolerable and military surplus parachutes were cheap. With a little work, a 28' Air Force back parachute could be made steerable, a sleeve could be added and D rings for the reserve attachment could be installed. At the urging of Parachutes Incorporated, Pioneer began to manufacture a line of sport equipment. Steve Snyder began work on an automatic opener designed to meet the particular requirements of the sport parachutist and to be named the "Sentinel". He incorporated as "Steve Snyder Enterprises" and filed a patent the following year.

Kittinger reached 702 mph in his plunge from 102,000 feet

1960. Captain Joseph W. Kittinger, Jr. stepped out of a balloon gondola at 102,000 feet over New Mexico with only a 6' stabilizing chute. During the freefall to 18,000 feet, he reached a terminal velocity of 702 mph.; the trip took four and a half minutes. Curt Hughes and Loy Brydon patented the famous TU steerable canopy modification. The Army parachutists swept the U.S. Team tryouts and competed in Sofia, Bulgaria. Barbara Gray of North Carolina and Sherrie Buck of California were the first female entries from the U.S.

1961. Ted Strong, coach of the West Point Parachute Team, returned to civilian life and established a parachute company in the Boston area. This was the year that the National Collegiate Parachuting League was established. In Orange, Massachusetts, four employees of Parachutes Incorporated, Jacques Istel, Lew Sanborn, Nate Pond and Bill Jolly, established two world records, the first for the U.S. . . . And, Pierre Lemoigne filed his basic Para-Sail/Para-Commander patent.

1962. The first PCA Instructor/Examiner Conference was held in Phoenix and 19 candidates took part. PCA membership was beginning to climb and had already reached 6,000. The U.S. hosted the 6th World Championships at Orange, Massachusetts; 24 nations were represented. For the first time, the U.S. fielded a full womens' team. After the meet, some northeast parachutists tried sleeving and jumping Lemoigne's Para-Sail. With the addition of some steering lines, Pioneer developed it into the Para-Commander. It was demonstrated at the 1964 Nationals in Issaquah, Washington, but conservative Pioneer was reluctant to market it.

1963. A combined Army and Air Force team bettered the Soviet Union's group altitude record of 37,000' when they exited a C-130 at 43,500' over El Centro, California. The Federal Aviation Administration published the first formal rules for sport parachuting thus recognizing the establishment of the activity. Lemoigne filed for another patent on the Para-Commander concept.

1964. Domina Jalbert of Boca Raton, Florida, filed for a patent on his ram air inflated Para Foil canopy. In the early part of the year, Loy Brydon helped Security develop the Crossbow (XBO) parachute system; the first sport piggyback, it was revolutionary. The canopy resembled the Para-Commander and its availability forced Pioneer to the market. The U.S. Team chose to use the PC in the XBO system and in 1964 they dazzled the World at the 7th W.P.C. In Leutkirch, West Germany. Six years after the first baton pass, six jumpers piled out of two aircraft over Arvin, California and formed the first six man star. Bob Buquor caught it all on film. This was the year the Chute Shop was established in Flemington, New Jersey. The Army Parachute Team made an assault on the world records and conquered 55% of them. This was the first time that any one nation had held a majority of them.

1965. The Arvin Good Guys formed the first eight man star. This year will also be well remembered for another reason as it was the time the commercial airline industry ganged up on the sport by encouraging the FAA to enact very restrictive regulations. Jumpers united under PCA and argued their case by writing letters and attending the hearing. The Air Transport Association and others didn't even bother to show up for the rebuttle session in the afternoon.

1967. The PCA is renamed the United States Parachute Association. The first ten man star was completed over Taft, California. A week later it was duplicated over Elsinore. Then six months later a ten man star competition was staged. In the 60's, most jumpers used non-steerable reserves in the belief that an ummodified canopy opened more reliably. Steerable modifications to reserve canopies hadn't been approved by the FAA and few people had them; well, few were known until the reserve was used. Toward the end of the decade, some lofts acquired approval for single or multiple "dog houses".

1968. Steve Snyder performed developmental work on the Para Wing and filed for a patent on his OSI or "Opening Shock Inhibitor", a heavy web strap which wrapped around the lines.

Johnny Carson receives his final equipment check prior to his first jump, a freefall from 12,500 feet.

The sport received a great deal of publicity that year when Bob Sinclair took Johnny Carson out at 12,500' on a buddy jump. Sinclair held the entertainer's harness until he pulled his ripcord. The video tape was shown on the "Tonight Show". Strong Enterprises developed the Stylemaster harness/container system for the U.S. Team. It incorporated a number of revolutionary design features.

1969. Steve Snyder began to market the Para-Plane, a ram air Jalbert canopy. He and Dick Morgan made an intense marketing effort to prove that a square canopy was superior to the round one for the accuracy event. As interest in relative work increased in the early 70's, many jumpers selected squares for their superior glide angle to get them back to the drop zone. The round, bulky PC was dead and the squares cornered the market except for some new light weight circular canopies. Snyder filed for a patent on his PCR or "Pilot chute Controlled Reefing" system.

1970. A four-man sequential relative work team event was introduced to the Nationals in Plattsburg, New York. Steve Snyder filed patents on a new ram air canopy suspension system and the Mark 2000 automatic opener.

1972. The ten-man event was introduced to the National Championships held in Tahlequah, Oklahoma. The name of the game was speed stars or forming the circle as soon as possible after exit. Interest developed in the team events and the biggest social event of the Winter jumping season was the Thanksgiving meet in Zephyrhills, Florida. The U.S. hosted the world championships in Tahlequah, Oklahoma.

1973. The Army Team's DC-3 crashed on the way to a demonstration jump killing all 14 aboard.

1974. A world record 31 man star was formed over Elsinore, California. North American Aerodynamics acquired the rights to the Jalbert Para Foil and began limited production. In the early 70's, relative work boomed and the buyer demanded parachutes which were smaller and lighter. Smaller meant the last team member would be closer to the door for the speed event. Lighter meant more freefall time since all would fall slower and a greater range of speed. Conventional systems were developed such as Strong's Fastback with a sloping top so it wouldn't hang up in the top of the door on exit and the POP TOP reserve which was very thin and clean. But by 1974, the equipment pendulum was swinging again and RW jumpers were returning to the piggyback; its clean lines made the flying better and slowed the fall. Jumpsuits grew bigger and bigger.

1975. A 32 man star was formed over Tahlequah and Snyder's Strato-Cloud went into production. About this time the FAA relaxed its insistance that manufacturers design and build entire parachute systems in order to acquire approval and this resulted in a great proliferation of small manufacturers producing harness/container assemblies specifically for the sport. Bill Booth eliminated the ripcord on his Wonderhog assembly and substituted

United States Patent [19]

Poynter

[11] **3,908,937**

[45] Sept. 30, 1975

[54] PARACHUTE PACK

[75] Inventor: **Daniel F. Poynter**, North Quincy, Mass.

[73] Assignee: **Strong Enterprises, Inc.,** North Quincy, Mass.

[22] Filed: Oct. 31, 1973

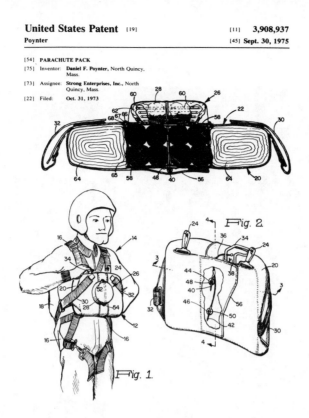

Fig. 2.

Fig. 1.

a throw out pilot chute. USPA moved its headquarters from Monterey, California, to Washington, D.C.

1976. The year of the U.S. bicentennial saw a new social event at the Nationals, the "Boogie". This was a four day affair between major jumping events filled with nonevaluated jumping, manufacturers' displays, seminars, canoe trips and fun. It was highly successful and promises to be an annual event.

1977. The large group event was changed from speed stars to sequential and team events became infinitely more popular than unaccompanied flight. Manufacturers catered to the relative worker. Ripcords were long ago changed from metal to plastic, the throw out pilot chute was very popular and many alternatives to the Capewell canopy releases appeared. Never before in the history of the parachute had so many users spent so much developmental effort without governmental fiscal inspiration.

1978. USPA membership continues to climb, the equipment becomes even more exotic and the sport continues its vigorous growth. More jumpers than ever become proficient at sequential relative work and canopy relative work becomes more popular.

CHAPTER IV
PARACHUTING EMERGENCIES
CAUSES, AVOIDANCE AND CURES

In the sport of parachuting there are a number of possible emergencies, happily all are rare. But since we are dealing with machines (aircraft), new elements (air and altitude), high closing speeds (terminal velocity approaching the ground), mechanical devices (parachutes), obstacles (trees, power lines, etc.), and last but certainly not least, the human element (you and your jumpmaster, pilot, instructor, et. al.), you must be educated in these areas, you must be properly prepared.

Emergency procedures are being given separate treatment here in their own chapter but they are not separate on the drop zone. They are mixed in with your other jump training. In the last chapter we told you to do a number of things such as to cover your reserve ripcord handle in the airplane. In this chapter we will explain in detail ''why''. Not all parachuting emergencies concern parachutes but all do concern parachuting. Injuries may be caused by a crash of the jump plane or canopy ride into an unexpected pond. In the following pages we will cover everything that can go wrong and what to do if it does.

Some statistics will help to orient our thinking. In the United States, over the last eight years, an annual average of 35 people have been fatally injured while parachuting. Nearly half of those who perished experienced a malfunction of their main canopy and then had problems deploying their reserve parachute. This category can be broken down further and there are some interesting explanations. 14% failed to pull the ripcord of either their main or reserve parachute. 9% were involved in collisions with other jumpers either doing relative work in freefall or in canopy collisions during opening. 9% pulled too low, 6% drowned, 2% landed in the powerlines, 2% died during landing and there were a few in the miscellaneous column. By one estimate, a fatality can be expected in one out of every 25,000+ jumps. At three jumps per day, this will take you quite some time. It should be pointed out that the above figures include *all* jumpers, both those who observe safety procedures and those who take chances. They even include some documented suicides. And it is interesting to compare numbers with other activities: last year over 200 people perished scuba diving, 900 bicycling, over 7,000 drowned, 1154 succumbed to bee stings, and 800 were even hit by lightning. Thousands of parachutists find jumping to be a great deal of fun; the ultimate outdoor, aviation recreation sport. You must weigh the risk and the reward; it's a personal decision.

There are also some interesting statistics on reserve use. One DZ reported 32 reserve openings out of 11,300 jumps. That works out to one out of every 354 jumps but it includes all types of equipment. The newer high performance canopies fail to deploy properly more often than the gear you are using; on student gear the reliability is much greater.

Canopy malfunctions and other emergencies are not common in sport parachuting but if one happens to you, once may be enough. Therefore, a disproportionate amount of discussion is being devoted to the problems here and a great deal of your training time will be expended on coping with them.

Emergency procedures will vary from drop zone to drop zone to fit local conditions. In fact, those lacking certain hazards may touch on the corrective action but lightly. Therefore, when visiting a new DZ, it is imperative that you get a briefing on the area.

In order to achieve the greatest enjoyment from your parachuting experience, you'll want to approach it with an unfogged mind. This means going to bed early the night before and lay off the booze. Even the common cold will trouble you due to the changes in atmospheric pressure. If your mind and body are not operating at 100%, you'll react with less deliberation in an emergency and you'll enjoy the jumping less.

It has been said that the difference between fear and respect is knowledge. Most people fear parachuting because they don't understand it. Fear is the result of ignorance and it is part of nature's protective mechanism; it warns us to beware when we are on unfamiliar ground. The best way to cope with problems is to prevent them in the first place. The key is education. It is unfortunate when someone is injured while engaging in sport but it is tragic when a second one is hurt for the same explainable reason.

AIRPLANE PROBLEMS. Engine and structural failures.

If the engine is going to fail, it will probably do so when the pilot reduces power after your full throttle takeoff. If it does, he'll attempt the best landing he can straight ahead off the end of the runway. Since you are helmeted, padded with gear and strapped in, you need only assume the proper position to be prepared. Draw your knees up, tuck your head down, fold your hands in back of your helmet and hold your head down to resist whiplash. As soon as

The "prepare-to-crash" attitude.

the plane comes to a stop, get out FAST! There is always the danger of fire, particularly if the aircraft has suffered structural damage on impact. Watch where you step, the plane may have clipped through some powerlines. They can zap you and they start grass fires.

Occasionally, the jump ship suffers a structural or other mechanical failure. Twisted-on parts sometimes twist off or a canopy may get draped over the tail jamming the controls.

Depending upon the situation and the altitude, your jumpmaster will select one of two commands: "PREPARE TO CRASH" or "GET OUT". The dividing line is usually set at 300m (1,000') above the ground since at this altitude there is enough time for an orderly exit and the pilot will probably be able to land his "glider" on the runway. The jumpmaster might tell you to jump and pull your reserve on the theory that it opens faster than the main.

"It is one thing to be in the proximity of death, to know more or less what she is, and it is quite another thing to seek her" — Ernest Hemingway.

So, if you're under 1,000', you'll land with the aircraft. If you are over 1,000' when the rubber band breaks, your jumpmaster will direct you to make a normal static line jump but you'll do it all a lot faster; swing out onto the step and go. Student freefallers may be directed to make a "jump and pull"; where they'll open their mains as soon as they clear the aircraft or the jumpmaster may sit them in the door, pull their reserve and simultaneously push them out. It all depends on the altitude at the time of the emergency. Licensed jumpers are next, then the jumpmaster and, in the case of severe structural failure, the pilot. The purpose of getting out of the plane is not only to remove you from the area of danger but to lighten the load making the aircraft easier to control. The jumpmaster goes next to last because he must take care of those in his charge. The pilot goes last (he wears a parachute too) so that he may wrestle the jumpship to keep it flying until you are gone.

Of course you will follow the instructions of your jumpmaster but sometimes you have to make the decision yourself. In the excitement of solving the engine or other problem, the pilot may allow the airspeed to drop, stalling the plane and allowing it to spin. In this condition the aircraft drops fast and the centrifugal force may pin you against the ceiling. Now is the time to scramble and get out.

Depending on the size of your jump ship and the procedure at your drop zone, your static line may be hooked up on the ground, at 300m (1,000') or on jump run. Whether or not your main is hooked up may determine what type of escape you can make in case of an aircraft emergency. For example, if you hook up prior to boarding, and the plane crashes on takeoff, when you unbuckle and get out, you can expect to unpack your main about three meters from the door (the length of your static line).

The final point to remember is to watch your jumpmaster for orders. When you receive them, carry them out quickly and without panic.

OPEN PARACHUTE IN THE AIRPLANE

Several times each year jumpers are pulled through the side of the jump plane when a container opens and a canopy escapes out the door. Only once has this resulted in a fatality but usually there is severe damage to both the jumper and the aircraft.

The jumper whose reserve escaped out the door of this aircraft was lucky, he survived. Notice how close he came to taking out the control cables which run through the door channel and just inside the torn Alclad.

If either the main or the reserve open prematurely in the aircraft, one of two things will happen: the pilot chute and/or canopy will either start out the door or remain in the plane. You have only one course of action for each situation.

"While it is rare, an airplane is a mere machine, and may therefore break" — J. Scott Hamilton.

Sometimes the main will burst open while you are in the back of the plane; the pins work their way out or the break cord snaps. In this case, it is a simple matter to move backward pinning the errant parachute against the bulkhead. Show the problem to your jumpmaster immediately. Once satisfied that you have it well secured, disconnect it from your harness by operating the canopy releases on your shoulders. If, somehow, it should get out the door later, you don't want to be connected to it. Now sit on it so it won't get away and ride the plane down.

Or perhaps since you were in the back of the plane, you weren't vigilantly guarding your reserve ripcord handle and it was snagged out as you moved around trying to find a comfortable position. Grab the reserve pilot chute and canopy and cover them, hold them tight. Call the jumpmaster's attention to the problem when you are sure the reserve isn't going anywhere, disconnect it from your harness. This includes disconnecting the Stevens Cutaway System if one is installed. Put the entire reserve in the rear of the cabin and sit on it.

Once the reserve starts out the door, it is impossible to retrieve.

You must follow it immediately. The decision has been made for you, you are going ready or not.

If, however, either of your canopies start out the door, you *will* follow it out. You have, at most, two seconds and if you hurry, you'll experience a near normal canopy ride to somewhere in the vicinity of the airport. But if you are slow, the developing canopy will act as a giant anchor, extracting you not through the door but, more than likely, through the side of the aircraft producing great injury to you both.

The best solution is prevention. Always guard and protect your ripcord handles.

Once the student leaves the step, he is on his own. There is no way the jumpmaster can close the gap to render assistance.

"It's usually the student we are worried about. He doesn't realize how dangerous that reserve ripcord handle can be when he gets near the door" — John Garrity.

DANGLING STATIC LINE

After the jumpmaster dispatches each student, he will unhook the static line and stow it in the back of the aircraft or under the pilot's seat. If he forgets to disconnect it, we have one ingredient for another horror story. During the scramble to exit, jumpers have managed to get these long pieces of webbing half-hitched around their ankle. The result is a surprising and abrupt halt just a short distance out the door. It is impossible to climb back up. There should be a knife in the plane to cut you loose and, of course, you should be carrying one. If there aren't any knives handy, you'll hope the pilot is sharp enough to think of breaking some glass out of one of the instruments in the panel because your alternatives are not terribly pleasant. Either you can pull your ripcord and jerk your leg off or you can wait it out and suffer severe "runway rash" when the plane lands. One jumper caught in this situation lucked out, he was jumping a helicopter. He was set down gently and red faced in front of everyone on the DZ.

PARACHUTE MALFUNCTIONS

A "malfunction" is any failure of the system to provide a normal rate of descent and this includes loss of canopy control. Malfunctions are normally caused by one or a combination of the following: bad packing, poor body position during canopy deployment and/or faulty equipment. Failures of the main parachute can be divided into two areas. Either nothing comes out and you have a "total malfunction" or the canopy opens but something is wrong with it and you have a "partial malfunction". Each of these two areas will be broken down still further in this chapter. According to recent USPA figures, if your main canopy malfunctions, there is an 89% chance it will be a "partial".

It is because of the possibility of an equipment malfunction that the opening altitude is set way up at 2500' (750m), why a second "reserve" parachute is worn and the reason you are drilled in its use. But even with the safety margin or "cushion", you must be aware of the time, speed and distances involved. As you exit the aircraft about 2500', you begin to accelerate; you start off at zero vertical speed and then fall faster and faster until you reach terminal velocity (more about that later). If you didn't have a parachute, it would take you about 18 seconds to reach the ground. In the case of a partial malfunction, you will have a little braking from your canopy and this means even more time. But even if you have a "total", allowing for reaction time, you should be open under your reserve at well above 1,000'. In fact, while it seemed like an eternity to you, your friends on the ground will tell you that you performed quickly and efficiently; you'll be surprised at how fast you react. Your main parachute takes 3-4 seconds to open and the reserve is just slightly faster. Even at terminal velocity, the fastest you can fall, four seconds translates into 700' (215m).

TOTAL MALFUNCTIONS

If you haven't been jerked upright by the sixth segment of your thousand count, you are already into the emergency procedure for a total malfunction. There are six types of totals and they will be covered in the order in which they might occur in a jump sequence.

"A chance is what you take before you think about it. A calculated risk is what you take after you have evaluated all possible factors and have determined that risk" — Craig Elliot

STUDENT IN TOW

One of the more dramatic problems is the static line hang up or "student in tow". It occurs when the jumper or some part of his equipment entangles with the static line preventing separation. He winds up suspended below the aircraft by the long nylon web. This one is extremely rare and if it does occur, it will probably be because the static line is misrouted (perhaps under the harness) and was missed in the equipment check or you and the jumpmaster failed to keep the line high and clear as you moved into the door to jump or because you performed some wild gymnastic maneuver instead of a stable exit and became entangled in it. Some students, despite all their training, yell "arch thousand" and then let go with the hands, leaving the feet firmly planted on the step and perform a back loop. The hang up presents all of you with a perplexing situation. The jump ship will be more difficult to fly, in fact, the pilot may be unable to maintain altitude because of all the extra drag. You don't want to land with the aircraft this way as even on the grass you'll suffer severe "runway rash". And you shouldn't pull your reserve because you don't know how the entanglement occurred; you don't know how you are attached. The static line might rip loose and, then again, it might rip you loose or you might all stay connected crashing the plane. As with other emergencies, there is an accepted procedure. You, your jumpmaster and pilot must be familiar with it.

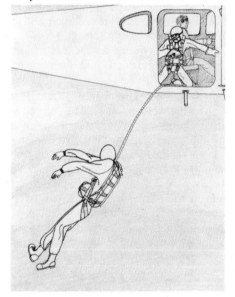

Conscious student in tow.

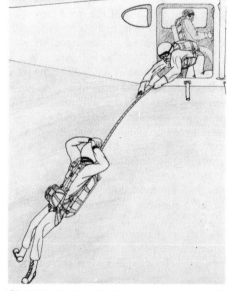

Signal the jumpmaster that you are prepared for him to cut the static line.

If you are conscious and your arms have not been injured, signal the jumpmaster so he'll know it is safe to cut you loose. The pilot will be diverting to a safer open area and will be trying to gain altitude. If you relax, you will probably assume a stable towing position either face or back to earth which is better than twisting slowly in the wind. Look up at your jumpmaster who will be holding up a knife for you to see indicating that he is ready to cut you loose. Place both hands on top of your helmet as a signal you understand the problem and are ready. Your jumpmaster will cut the static line, as you fall away, follow the procedure for a total malfunction: pull and punch. Be sure you're cut loose before you pull the reserve.

The unconscious student in tow.

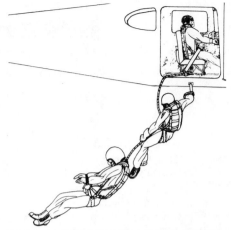

The jumpmaster attaches himself to the static line with a snap link and lowers himself toward the unconscious student.

Gripping the main lift web of the student's harness just above the D ring installation, he cuts the static line.

As both fall away free, the jumpmaster pulls the student's reserve ripcord and then pushes him away. Then he pulls his own ripcord.

If, however, you are unconscious or otherwise incapacitated, you won't be able to give the OK signal to your jumpmaster and he will elect an alternative procedure. The pilot will head for a large open area and the jumpmaster will check his equipment. Then the jumpmaster will sit in the door, attach a snap link between his harness and your static line and let himself gently down the line. Coming to rest at about your shoulder level, he will reach over your shoulder with his left hand to firmly grip your main lift web just above where the reserve D ring is attached. Once set, he will draw his knife and sever the line. As you drop away together, he will discard the knife and simultaneously pull your reserve and push you away. As your parachute begins to deploy, he will pull his own ripcord.

There is another interesting method of dealing with unconscious students in tow which should be mentioned as it is in use at some drop zones. With the addition of some extra hardware and straps, the jumpmaster will attach his reserve to your static line and then cut it all loose. The result is that the student descends under a reserve canopy, attached to it by the static line.

Many years back, this Army test jumper managed to hang his canopy over the tail. A knife was lowered to him from a second plane. He cut himself free and opened his reserve. (The canopy release was a later development).

There is also a second type of in-tow emergency to be considered: via the main canopy. You fall away from the step so quickly that it is virtually impossible to tangle your canopy in the tail but if one of your parachutes opens when you are on the step, entanglement may occur. If you find yourself in this situation look at your reserve ripcord, jettison your main via your shoulder mounted canopy releases and pull your reserve immediately.

STATIC LINE NOT HOOKED UP

Occasionally, despite all procedures, a student exits the jump plane without being attached to it. While hooking up the static line is the jumpmaster's responsibility, you also have a great interest in it. If you forgot to check and find yourself in freefall, follow the procedure for a total: pull and punch.

HARD PULL

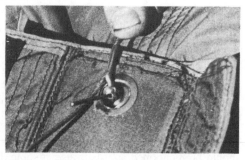

A top pin unprotected by a stiffener and cover may be caught in the top of the door and bent.

Once you graduate to freefall, you may from time to time experience a "hard pull". It may be caused by bent or deeply seated ripcord pins, the lack of sufficient supporting canopy inside the top of the container, a loose or dirty cone, an unbalancing pressure from the pilot chute (cone lock), a pigtail in the ripcord cable, etc. If you feel resistance to your pull, give it two quick trys with both hands on the handle and then if that doesn't do it, pull your reserve ripcord. After a number of jumps, it's normal to become somewhat complacent about the pull; you may give it a relaxed, half-hearted jerk. It may take as much as 10 kg (22 lbs.), so pull again. If continual hard pulls are bothering you, wax your pins by drawing them over a candle (or a waxy Coke cup from the trash barrel). It will make quite a difference though it will only last for 2-3 jumps and you will have to do it again.

FLOATING RIPCORD

The floating ripcord.

Another freefall problem is the floating ripcord. The tacking securing the end of the housing to the harness may come loose and the handle may come out of its pocket, blowing up behind you. Look for it, reach for the housing on your shoulder and follow it back to the handle. But don't waste time with it. If you can't locate the handle immediately, dump your reserve.

PACK CLOSURE.

Sometimes after pulling we experience a pack closure. Somehow, all the forces of bow stiffeners, pilot chute springs, pack opening bands, etc. seem to balance out and the side flaps of the pack just don't part. A swift and well placed elbow may jar it loose. If not, dump the reserve. Don't waste time, you don't know what is causing the problem.

PILOT CHUTE HESITATION.

Another freefall problem encountered at pull time is the common pilot chute hesitation or "burble". This is when the pilot chute momentarily flutters in the low pressure area behind you rather than catching air. It's not likely to happen before you graduate to freefall because your static line is connected to your pilot chute with Velcro or breakcord which will pull it out. The burble may be caused by a bent pilot chute spring, poor pilot chute placement, etc. but usually it is just sitting in the dead air space created behind you when you are in the spread stable position. Sometimes it jumps upon release but fails to travel far enough to get a grip on the air rushing past you. It may drop back down and just bounce around or even lay there. It is very common and will be corrected when you bend over to pull your reserve since

---

"As in all emergencies, it would be wrong to think that they happen on every flight but it would be foolish not to prepare for them" — Charles Shea-Simonds

when you bend, the air flow around you will change. If you leave the left hand out and bring the right hand in to grasp the reserve ripcord handle, you will turn on your right side allowing the airflow to get at the pilot chute and pull it free. After a while, you may subconsciously develop the habit of peeking over your shoulder after pulling the ripcord or you may sit up to dump. This method of pulling in the start of a backloop also reduces the opening forces. These are techniques you may wish to adopt later, as you gain skill in maneuvering in freefall.

In case of a total malfunction, pull the reserve immediately.

DEALING WITH THE TOTAL

Of all the possible equipment malfunctions, the ''total'' is the easiest to deal with because there is no other garbage over your head to interfere with the deploying reserve. While you are on static line, all you have to remember is to pull and punch. Later you will want to refine the drill by throwing away your main ripcord so it won't tangle in the lines of the deploying reserve and you'll bend forward at the waist with the feet together to bring you over on your back for a cleaner opening. It is also wise to raise your left arm to cover and protect the canopy releases and your face from the fast moving reserve. So while the total is the easiest malfunction to rectify, remember that it also presents you with the least amount of time in which to act. When in doubt, whip it out!

When dealing with a total, do not waste any time by attempting to first jettison the main canopy. Some will argue that they want to avoid the possibility of an entanglement caused if the main should belatedly begin to deploy simultaneously with the reserve. Time is precious and the chance of entanglement not too great. If your main starts out, let it go. Your rate of descent under two canopies will be just about the same as under one because both are tipped and spilling air. In any case, you won't have the ability to steer. If you like, you may activate your canopy releases to jettison the main after both canopies are completely inflated and a visual inspection of the reserve canopy satisfies you that it is intact.

PARTIAL MALFUNCTIONS

A partial malfunction is one in which the canopy comes out of the container but does not properly deploy. It may not inflate (e.g. a streamer which hardly slows your descent at all) or it may take on some air (e.g. a cigarette roll which will probably slow you enough for a safe landing). So, partial malfunctions may be major and minor. An additional important consideration is that they may be stable or spinning. Most partials can usually be attributed

---

''Passing through two grand at terminal with nothing out is not the time or place to be paging through this book'' — Curt Curtis.

to an error in packing or poor body position on opening.

If you want to start a discussion, inquire as to the best method of reserve deployment under a partial. The USPA recommends two methods; in order of preference, they are (1) the breakaway and (2) manually controlled deployment of the reserve parachute. The breakaway is recommended over the manually controlled because it consists of a single simple procedure which applies to all partial malfunctions, stable or spinning, while the manually controlled technique requires proficiency in several variations of procedure, depending on the type of malfunction and type of equipment. The throw out method is part of our airborne troop heritage. They exit much lower to avoid enemy fire and don't have the altitude required for a breakaway. As a student, you will subscribe to the breakaway method if you are equipped with a Stevens Cutaway System. The SCS has a line attaching your risers to your reserve ripcord handle so that all you need to do is to jettison the main via the canopy releases; the reserve is pulled quickly and automatically. Later, when you progress to a higher performance canopy, which often rotate violently when they malfunction, you will want to breakaway. Both the manual deployment and breakaway procedures are described in detail in a few more pages.

| STREAMER | PACK CLOSURE | PARTIAL INVERSION ("MAE WEST") | BLOWN PANELS | GOOD |

These are some of the canopies you could see when you look up over your shoulder on the fifth count.

LINE TWISTS

Line twists are so common and easy to correct they hardly qualify as a malfunction. Sometimes, the canopy spirals a few turns as it lifts off and you find it difficult to get your head back so you can look up at the canopy. The risers are close together and twisted instead of spread. Simply reach above your head, grab the risers and spread them to accelerate the untwisting. While you have them spread, check your canopy to make sure nothing else is wrong with it.

LINE TWISTS

Blown panels.

BLOWN PANELS AND TEARS

A few blown panels are usually not a great concern. In fact, many students don't even notice them because they expect to see large cut out sections in the steerable canopy. A lot of

"Students are generally not aware of how quickly 20 seconds pass" — Betsy Robson.

nylon has already been removed to make the canopy steerable, some more won't increase the rate of descent much but it may slow the forward speed depending on the location of the damage. Tears, even large ones and the odd broken line do not require use of the reserve either. So there is no hard, fast rule; the decision is entirely yours.

CIGARETTE ROLL

The cigarette roll is unique. Somehow, during inflation, the lower lateral band begins to roll tightly upward fusing the nylon. Unless it is combined with a partial inversion, most of the canopy will probably remain and reserve activation will not be required.

STREAMER

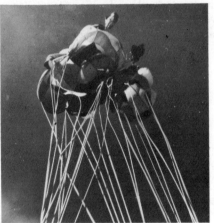

The Streamer

The streamer or "roman candle" occurs where the deployment device (sleeve or bag) fails to come off of the canopy or where it does let out the canopy but the canopy fails to spread. You may be pulled upright but it doesn't slow your fall very much so time is of the essence. You don't want to waste time tugging on the main to encourage it to open, it's time for the reserve.

HORSESHOE

The horseshoe

The horseshoe malfunction is where the top of the canopy becomes entangled with the jumper or his equipment causing the canopy and suspension lines to form a loop above the falling jumper. The pilot chute may be caught on a boot bracket, pack opening band, foot etc. or sometimes a student performs a particularly wild exit and traps the pilot chute under his arm. Sometimes the horseshoe is momentary and can be cleared, leaving the canopy free to inflate. But watch the altitude, if you can't shake or pull it off immediately, go for the reserve.

PARTIAL INVERSION

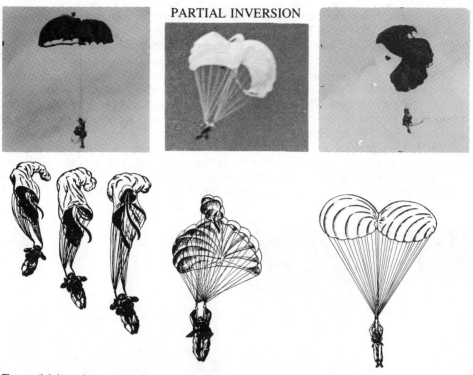

The partial inversion occurs when part of the skirt blows inward and goes under the skirt on the opposite side. The result is much less drag area and a faster rate of descent.

If the resulting lobes are of equal size, it may be called a "Mae West".

The partial inversion or Mae West gets its name because it takes on the appearance of a large brassiere. It is a malfunction where part of the canopy near the skirt inverts on deployment to form a small pocket. One side of the canopy becomes inverted and it is greatly reduced in size increasing the descent rate. Due to the imbalance it causes, the canopy may begin to spin and the longer it spins, the faster it goes. If the skirt continues its movement between the lines on the other side, the partial inversion may progress into a "full inversion" with the canopy completely in-side-out. Your lines will be crossed, the pilot chute will be hanging down on the inside of the canopy and steering will be backwards. It is speculated that the partial inversion is caused by an uneven skirt. This may happen when one shoulder is lower than the other or because you failed to straighten the apex when packing. You are probably turning and descending fast so it's reserve time again.

DEALING WITH PARTIAL MALFUNCTIONS.
THE MANUALLY CONTROLLED "THROW-OUT" PROCEDURE.

The throw-out procedure requires that the reserve parachute be activated and the canopy deployment be controlled by hand while the parachutist remains attached to his malfunction-

"Student emergency procedures should be as simple as possible. If it is rather complicated for a student to understand and perform on a jump, it will be difficult to teach, the student will be more unsure of his ability, and the student will be more likely to make a mistake during an actual emergency" — Don Grant.

ing main canopy. Its proponents cite several advantages, among them the lack of a requirement for extra, special equipment and the theory that "something is better than nothing". (That you still have some support from your malfunctioned main if you fail to correctly deploy your reserve.) However, others will cite some disadvantages such as the lengthy training sessions required, the confusing and complex procedures, the need to learn a new procedure when graduating to a high performance canopy and the possibility of a main-reserve entanglement. The throw-out method has been around for years, we inherited it from the Airborne. But their situation is different in that they are exiting much lower to avoid enemy fire. The don't have time for a breakaway. In fact, in combat, they exit so low, they rarely have time for reserves at all. Most will agree, however, that the throw-out method is a satisfactory procedure when the student is properly trained and supervised.

If you are subscribing to the manually controlled procedure, your reserve must not be equipped with a pilot chute as it will increase the chances of entanglement.

Skratch Garrison demonstrates the throw-out under his good canopy. He pulls and discards the ripcord and lifts out the canopy.

And throws it vigorously out, down and to the side.

Then feeds out the suspension lines hand over hand.

And the canopy fully inflates.

Now he has a choice of riding both down, jettisoning the main or hauling down the reserve by pulling on one line hand over hand.

In the manually controlled category, you must recognize the malfunction, make a decision on the procedure to use and then act on it.

"One of the great attractions of the sport to many of us is that it demands competence and skillful decision making under pressure" — J. Scott Hamilton.

Type malfunction	Importance to Student	Student actions
1. Total (no drag)	fast descent/no parachute/17-19 seconds to act.	pull and punch quickly.
2. Streamer or Horseshoe (low drag)	fast descent/low drag from parachute/17-19 seconds to act.	pull and scoop reserve away from body and main quickly. Throw away to avoid main entanglement.
3. Partial (some drag)	some drag/probably will spin/descent faster than usual/could get worse.	control the reserve. Throwout, down, in direction of spin.
4. Minor problems (full drag)	full drag/lost toggle/line twists/good rate of descent/minor difficulty.	use your head but if in doubt, whip it out!

The USPA recommended procedure for manually controlled reserve deployment is as follows:

1, Observe the malfunction immediately after "opening".

2, Make a quick attempt to clear the malfunction if there is time and then make the decision to activate the reserve.

3, Throw away the main ripcord. They have a way of tangling in the lines of a deploying canopy.

4, Cross your legs to reduce the possibility of entanglement with canopy and suspension lines.

5, Place your left hand over the reserve ripcord pin protector flap with your palm facing your stomach and thumb up.

6, Pull the reserve ripcord with the right hand and throw it away.

7, Roll the left hand, which is covering the pin flap, outward allowing the reserve container to open exposing the canopy. Hold the canopy in place.

8, Place the right hand under the top flap of the reserve container, around and under the canopy with the fingers and thumb pointing down. Get a good grip on the canopy and stretch it out to arms' length freeing a couple of line stows.

9, Lift the canopy up to the side of your head and vigorously throw it down, out, away and in the same direction as the spin. It should begin to scoop air, inflating and taking shape.

10, Assist the canopy in unstowing the lines if necessary. If it won't inflate but just flops down by your legs, this is a sign that you aren't descending fast enough to need it. If you are descending rapidly, the reserve canopy will inflate rapidly and by itself.

11, Once the canopy is inflated, you may jettison the main canopy by activating your shoulder mounted canopy releases.

12, Look around and prepare to land.

THE BREAKAWAY PROCEDURE

The breakaway or "cutaway" is an emergency procedure which involves jettisoning the main canopy prior to deploying the reserve. This is contra to the "something is better than nothing" theory but experience has shown the breakaway to be simpler to learn, easier to execute and more succssful when properly performed. Jumpers with high performance

"Out of 10,000 feet of fall, always remember that the last half inch hurts the most" — Capt. Charles W. Purcell, 1932.

canopies should use the breakaway since they are likely to be rotating violently with a partial malfunction. And the procedure should be implemented without delay as the revolutions may increase in speed creating a great deal of centrifugal force making arm movement difficult. Those subscribing to the breakaway method should have their reserve equipped with a spiral spring type pilot chute and a launching disc (see the equipment chapter). Today, most experienced jumpers are using piggyback parachute assemblies where both the main and reserve are worn on the back. They have no choice and are committed to the breakaway since they can't get their hands on the reserve canopy to throw it out manually. Harnesses are equipped with canopy releases; the older ones with the Capewell brand and the newer ones with modifications to the Capewell and some interesting light weight alternatives. The canopy releases must be suitable for the breakaway. Student chest reserves and some piggybacks are equipped with a reserve static line arrangement. The Stevens Cutaway System consists of two cross straps connecting the main risers and a line from one riser to the reserve ripcord handle. Its purpose is to eliminate one of the motions in the breakaway sequence: pulling the reserve. Since half a breakaway is worse than no breakaway at all, it shouldn't be left up to an inexperienced parachutist.

The SCS in use. Note the short distance between the jettisoned main and the reserve canopy.

The SCS usually produces full deployment of the reserve canopy in less than 30 meters (100'). If you find a static line system when you graduate to a piggyback harness/container assembly, you should leave it on. But after a number of jumps, you may choose to dispense with the SCS on your chest mounted reserve so you won't have to hook and unhook the line all the time. When you and your instructor develop enough confidence that you will pull the reserve after a breakaway, you can do away with the line but you should keep the cross connector straps since they guard you against the danger of a canopy release hang up.

The decision altitude for the breakaway method is 550m (1800'). This is your safety margin, above this it is safe to try to clear the malfunction but at this point, all clearing work must stop. Watch your altitude. The breakaway must be commenced above 500m(1600') to assure you plenty of time to get the reserve out. Under high speed malfunctions you may be just seven seconds off the deck at this point and it may be necessary to forget the breakaway and just pull the reserve.

"Fatality data seem to indicate that conversion training is often poor to nonexistent when people graduate to piggyback systems and exotic canopies" — J. Scott Hamilton.

To breakaway with a chest mounted reserve, straighten and spread the legs (for lateral stability) and pull them straight up in front. Bend the back, roll the shoulders forward and pull the head forward. On release, you will fall into a stable, back to earth "rocking chair" position.

To breakaway with the back mounted reserve, spread the legs (for lateral stability and push them back as far as possible while bending the knees about 45 degrees (only). Arch the back and pull your head back but keep the chin resting on the chest. On release you will fall into a stable, face to earth position.

Body position is very important. If you are not falling away correctly, you may become entangled in the canopy and/or lines of your deploying reserve.

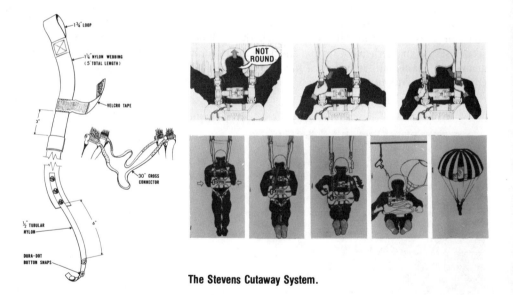

The Stevens Cutaway System.

As a student, you will only use the breakaway method if your parachutes are equipped with a Stevens Cutaway System. And there are a couple of things that you must understand about it. With the SCS you are totally committed to the breakaway because your reserve has a pilot chute installed. You cannot safely deploy the reserve canopy without first getting rid of the main. And you must always treat the SCS as a back up to the breakaway. It is not an automatic device placed there to rescue you from all known dangers. After jettisoning the main, you must attempt to pull the reserve. It isn't likely you will beat the line but you must try and this try must be part of your training drill.

The breakaway procedure is as follows:

1, Observe the canopy immediately after "opening".

2, If there is a streamer, breakaway immediately. If you are low, just pull the reserve; there isn't time to jettison the main.

3, If you have a partial, check your altitude and if above 1800', try to clear it. Sometimes you can pull down on a line and sometimes a pull on a steering toggle will do it. Don't spend a lot of time on this.

4, Make the decision to breakaway.

5, Throw away the main ripcord. They have been known to tangle in the lines of a deploying reserve.

6, Remove the safety cover on both riser releases and look at the reserve ripcord handle.

7, Assume the proper body position.

8, Breakaway using a strong hammer-like thrust rotating the latches out and down. If one hangs up, use two hands on it.

9, Quickly bring the left hand across the chest to the right shoulder, protecting the open canopy releases (they're tangly) and, at the same time, reach for the reserve ripcord with the right hand.

10, Pull the reserve ripcord. If you have an SCS, the ripcord should be gone already. If you have a center pull reserve, it may be necessary to hold the pack down with the left forearm as you pull with the right hand. If you don't have an SCS and did pull the reserve, throw the ripcord away to the side. The pilot chute should jump 2-3 meters from the pack before it spreads to catch air drawing the canopy out. Brace yourself for the opening.

11, Check your reserve canopy, look around and prepare to land.

Breakaway training is essential to assure that it will be accomplished completely, quickly and well. This must be done in a suspended harness which is easy to rig up. Simply tie an old set of risers to an overhead beam and attach them to your harness. The drill must be repeated again and again until it becomes mechanical and automatic so that you will perform correctly and without hesitation.

TWO CANOPIES OPEN

Sometimes the reserve opens accidentally or the main reinflates presenting you with two canopies.

"Aviation is not in itself inherently dangerous. But to even a greater degree than even the sea, it is terribly unforgiving of any carelessness, incapacity or neglect" —

You may find yourself confronted with two fully open canopies; this can happen in several ways. The most common cause in the initial jumps is where the student grabs the reserve handle instead of the dummy main ripcord. Another is reacting very quickly to a pilot chute hesitation and there are some freaky ones. One jumper tied a lanyard to his boot mounted smoke generator and taped it to his leg so he wouldn't have to reach all the way to his foot to activate the smoke. He exited the aircraft, pulled the smoke and deltaed for the star forming below. He forgot about the lanyard and didn't notice that it was entangled in his gloved hand and streaming upward. When he reached in to pull his main ripcord, the line whipped around his reserve handle. His pull activated both parachutes.

If the two canopies take off at different times, they probably won't tangle with each other and two canopies will descend at about the same rate as one but steering becomes impossible. So if your automatic opener blows after your main is open and the reserve starts out, grab it and stick it between your knees to free your hands for steering. You may elect to jettison the main canopy or haul down the reserve canopy depending on which one is in better shape, is more steerable and is easier to accomplish. The reserve may be hauled in by pulling down on a single line hand over hand until the skirt is reached. At this point it will collapse and deflate so roll it up and stick it between your legs. Time is short, pulling down the reserve requires strength and the lines will seem to cut into your hands so you'll only have one chance at it.

Jettison the malfunctioned main canopy.

Or pull down the reserve canopy and stick it between your legs.

Hanging under just your reserve you'll probably find yourself in an uncomfortable feet forward position because it is attached to your harness below your chest. Reach through the groups of suspension lines pulling yourself upright and route them under your arms and behind your shoulders.

MALFUNCTIONED RESERVE

Perhaps you have jettisoned your main only to find yourself with a malfunctioned reserve canopy. It certainly is not your day! Or perhaps you want to advise a pilot friend in the use of his single parachute. Here are some of the problems and suggested procedures:

Streamer: Pull down on a couple of lines to move the apex vent off center.

Partial inversion: Pull down on the lines attached to the lower side of the inversion.

73

PULL DOWN ON LINES ATTACHED TO LOWER SIDE OF INVERSION "8," AS SHOWN. THE INVERSION WILL SLIP OUT.

NOTE THAT ONE PART OF THE SKIRT OF THE PARACHUTE IS LOW AT THE CROSS-OVER OF THE "8."

PULLING DOWN ON THE LOW LOOP OF THE "8" TURNS THE LOOP IN THE DIRECTION OF THE ARROW.

The technique for removing a partial inversion.

Blown panels: There is nothing you can do short of climbing up on top of the canopy with a sewing machine but, like tears and the odd broken line, they won't greatly affect the rate of descent. In fact, they just may make the canopy more stable.

LANDING PROBLEMS

Most of your landings will be normal and in the center of the drop zone but unusual things do happen like landing in water, in sudden high winds or descending through power lines. High winds were covered in the chapter on your first jump, other landing problems are covered here.

TREE LANDINGS

To protect yourself in a tree landing, press your legs together and cross your arms to cover your face and throat.

74

The tree landing is rarely hazardous. Your canopy will lower you gently into and through the tree as you slow further, breaking the thinner branches. You will probably go all the way through to the ground and make a normal PLF (parachute landing fall).

If you can't avoid the trees, face into the wind to minimize your ground speed and place your feet and knees tightly together so you won't straddle a branch. Place the left arm over the eyes and the left hand in the right armpit, palm outward. Place the right arm across the left arm and the right hand in your left armpit, palm outward. Turn your head to the side and down to protect your face and throat. Hold this position as you descend through the branches. Do not attempt to brake your descent by grasping limbs, you are better off going all the way through to the ground slowly than ending up sitting in the top of the tree. Prepare for a PLF. If you come to rest short of the ground, check your position. If close, release from your harness and drop down. If you are up quite a ways, relax and wait for help. Keep your helmet on until you have both feet firmly on the ground. Its purpose is to protect your head from takeoff to touchdown and you aren't down yet.

If help does not arrive, you may have to climb down yourself. Perhaps you are way off the DZ and dusk is approaching. It's hard to shout continually and it is nice to have a whistle in times like these. You may pop the reserve, let down the canopy and lines and then climb down hand over hand. If you let the narrow nylon lines slip through your fingers and aren't wearing gloves, you will receive painful friction burns so go hand over hand. Be sure you are climbing down the *outside* of the canopy. Those who have made the mistake have spent the night trapped inside a canopy dangling from a tree.

WATER LANDINGS

Unintentional water landings are the most dangerous of all.

There are two types of water jumps, those you plan and those you don't. An intentional water jump is an exciting, rewarding combination of aviation and water sports. But being unexpectedly blown out over the lake is cause for great concern. In fact, while only *one* jumper has perished in a planned water jump in the last eight years, 19 have drowned in unexpected water landings.

The procedures for these two very different types of landings are not the same. In an intentional water landing, you will slide back in the saddle, swing the reserve, undo the chest and one leg strap and release the last leg snap upon splashing down. This procedure is also recommended if you find yourself being blown unexpectedly out over the ocean or other immense body of water. When there is absolutely no question that you are going for a dunking, you should get out of your gear, but this procedure should not be followed unless you are sure you are going in, planned or otherwise.

When one is making an intentional water jump, conditions are good, the jump is planned and the necessary equipment is worn. The ingredients for tragedy, on the other hand, are born by the unprepared for the unexpected.

The Basic Safety Regulations require the carrying of flotation gear when parachuting within one mile of any water deep enough to take a life but there are times when one mile is not enough. A bad spot on a big load with high upper winds, sudden radical wind changes, a popped reserve as you exit at twelve grand, for examples, may carry you far from the friendly DZ. And some water requires more protection than just flotation gear, such as when one punches through the ice in the middle of a lake.

Most unintentional water landings are also unexpected. They take place in narrow rivers and small ponds, so small that one usually doesn't know for sure that he is going in until just a short distance from splash-down. There is no time to swing the reserve, slide back in the saddle and undo the snaps, particularly if the jumper is trying to avoid trees at the time. As a result, he is going into the water in all his gear and his chances are poor.

On the other hand, if he does go through the water landing procedure "just in case" and then misses the water only to land in the trees because he couldn't spend enough time steering, he may fall out of his harness, subjecting himself to other dangers.

The greatest danger in water landings is becoming entangled in the net-like canopy. In fact, we should think of "panic, canopy, drowning". All are very different but very much related and one leads to the other. If there is little wind in the small tree protected pond, the canopy will deflate and fall straight down on the jumper in a hugh mess of tangled nylon fabric and lines. If he panics, he is sure to become caught in the trap. It seems logical, then, to try to avoid the canopy.

The procedure recommended for unintentional water landings is as follows: You are at 300 meters (or 1,000') and the wind is backing you toward a water hazard. If you continue to face the wind, you may land short of it and if you turn to run, you may land on the other side of it but one thing is for sure: you will land in the vicinity of it. So, reach down and sling your reserve by unsnapping the belly band on one side and unhooking one reserve snap. At double to triple the height of the trees, face into the wind to minimize your ground speed, uncover both canopy releases and place your feet and knees firmly together. Continue to steer and then just before touchdown, reach for the canopy releases. At the moment your feet get wet, not one moment sooner, activate the releases. The tensioned canopy will recoil upwards and even a mild wind will carry it away. Altitude is very difficult to judge, especially over flat ground or a large body of water. One is always tempted to drop out of the harness "just before" touching down, but what appears to be just a "leg length" may really be building height.

This procedure will leave you floating with your harness and reserve on but with the dangerous canopy gone. Roll over on your back and take off the reserve and/or the harness. Actually, the harness won't hurt or restrict you and the reserve will even provide positive flotation for a minute or so. In fact, the reserve won't become negatively buoyant for about three minutes. So, just unsnap the reserve and use it for a life preserver.

If the canopy does land on top of you anyway, grab it and "walk" a radial seam to the skirt. There is no reason to panic as you can always lift the porous fabric to form a space to breathe. Once clear of the canopy, swim away using mostly the hands until you are clear of the lines.

One planned water jump is required for the USPA Class D Expert license. This requirement has probably saved hundreds of lives as it has provided water landing familiarization to thousands. If you should land in a river, even a slow moving one, you want to

---

"Water can be fun or terribly inhospitable. Like fire, one must be careful with it and then it should only be taken in small doses" — Jack Bergman

jettison your main as soon as possible. If it catches in the current, it will drag you under and downstream away from your rescuers.

Besides your reserve, certain other pieces of your gear may provide some flotation. Pneumatic soled jump boots, full shell helmets, knotted jumpsuits, etc., they are all there for those who think to use them.

POWERLINE LANDINGS

You must avoid powerlines at all cost, the danger is just too great. Look for the high tension wires. If you are at an unfamiliar DZ or land off target, look for poles, wires run between them invisibly. Keep them continually in mind from the time you open so you can avoid them. High tension lines don't look so dangerous but they strike with the speed and power of lightning. They may electrocute you in an instant or put you in the hospital with severe burns; it isn't at all pleasant. If there is any question about clearing the lines, turn and run with the wind until you are past them and make the decision high enough.

If landing in the wires is inevitable, it is essential that you avoid touching more than one wire at a time. Any bird will tell you that it takes two wires to get zapped.

Avoid touching more than one powerline at a time.

Leave the canopy retrieval to the power company.

If you are going into the wires, face your canopy into the wind to minimize ground speed and make your final descent as close to vertical as possible. Place your feet and knees firmly together with the toes pointed to avoid straddling a wire. Extend your arms overhead with the elbows straight and palms against the front risers. Look for wires and wriggle and squirm as necessary trying to avoid touching more than one at a time. If you come to rest near the ground, jettison the canopy quickly and get away. If you stop above jumping height, keep very still and wait for help. Over 600 volts, nylon becomes a conductor and any movement on your part may force a contact.

Once you get to the ground, be alert for broken powerlines, they are like snakes hidden in the grass and they not only strike, they sometimes start fires. Never pull on a canopy attempting to remove it from the wires, it may be your very last good deed. Let the power company do it, it's their kind of work.

As we said in the beginning, avoid powerlines by thinking about them from the time you open. There is no excuse not to.

OTHER OBSTACLES

There are many other landing obstacles which are potentially hazardous to parachutists

"Go directly to Malfunction Junction: do not pass GO, do not collect $200." — (overheard in Atlantic City).

such as ditches, fences, hard roads and even some unique ones like hot water geysers. These hazards at your DZ will be pointed out to you in your first jump course, probably with a marked aerial photograph. When visiting a new drop zone, be sure to check in with an instructor or the Club Safety Officer for a briefing on their local hazards and recommended alternate landing areas.

When you are in the air, look for the danger areas. Fences run between visible fence posts, powerlines run between power poles, isolated buildings are serviced by electricity. Powerlines, ditches, and fences often border roads, airplanes land on runways, etc. It's easy but it's all new and the approach is different; you are looking down at the terrain, not horizontally.

If an obstacle presents itself, steer your canopy to avoid it. Turn your canopy to "run" and land beyond it, if necessary. Successful landings under a parachute are like those in an airplane: the ones you walk away from are "good". It is far better to land outside the target area and walk back than land on a fence and be carried back. If you pass over the obstacle very low, you may not have sufficient altitude to turn into the wind. It is then preferable to crab the canopy slightly and try to do your best PLF. But, obviously, the best solution is to think and plan ahead to avoid the obstacle in the first place.

AIRPORT SAFETY

Never smoke around aircraft, hangers or pumps. The combination of aviation fuel and aircraft dope present a great fire risk. When moving light aircraft, be careful where you push. They are covered with very light fabric or metal and are easy to damage. The pilot will show you where it is safe to apply pressure.

Beware of the prop! It is difficult to see and will make quick mince meat of anyone who walks into it. Always walk around the back of the plane, never the front. Get into the habit. Leave the dog and the children at home, the airport is not a nursery. Stand where the taxiing pilot can see you, his visibility is not good.

If your airport has more than one runway, stay off the "active". It will normally be the one running the closest to the direction of the wind. Remember that planes usually takeoff and land into the wind and look for them up there. Rules change from airport to airport and at some you will not be allowed to cross the active.

Be nice to the pilots, they have a lot of clout on the airport and you may need one to fly the jumpship. Be patient with the whuffos (spectators), they *are* public opinion.

UNITED STATES PARACHUTE ASSOCIATION PUBLICATIONS
PART 100—BASIC SAFETY REGULATIONS

SUBPART A—GENERAL

100.01 Applicability
(a) This Part prescribes rules governing all parachute jumps made in the United States, except:
1. Parachute jumps necessary because of an in-flight emergency; and
2. Parachute jumps made while under military orders to perform such jumps when these orders require that the parachute jump be of a nature contrary to these regulations.
(b) For the purpose of this Part, a "parachute jump" means the descent of a person to the surface from an aircraft in flight when he intends to use, or uses, a parachute during all or part of that descent.

"Anyone who hates dogs and children, can't be all bad" – An airport operator, with apologies to W.C. Fields.

(c) All persons participating in parachuting should be familiar with:

1 Part 10, USPA Publications (Definitions);

2 Part 100, USPA Publications (these regulations);

3 Part 101, USPA Publications (Waivers to the BSR's);

4 Part 104, USPA Publications (USPA Licenses);

5 USPA Doctrine; and

6. All Federal, State and local regulations and rules pertaining to parachuting.

100.11 Compliance with Regulations

No parachute jump shall be made in violation of Federal Aviation Administration regulations.

SUBPART B—ADMINISTRATIVE

100.13 Medical Requirements

All persons engaging in parachuting shall:

(a) Carry a valid Class I, II or III Federal Aviation Administration Medical Certificate; or

(b) Carry a certificate of physical fitness for parachuting from a registered physician; or

(c) Have completed the USPA Medical Certificate.

100.15 Age Requirements

Civilian parachutists shall be at least:

(a) the age of legal majority (to execute contracts); or

(b) 16 years of age with notarized parental or guardian consent.

SUBPART C—OPERATIONS

100.21 Novice Parachutists

(a) All novice instruction shall be under the supervision of a currently rated USPA Instructor or USPA Instructor/Examiner.

(b) All novice parachute jumps must be made under the direct supervision of a currently rated USPA Jumpmaster aboard the aircraft until the novice has been certified by his CSO, ASO, USPA Instructor or USPA Instructor/Examiner to jumpmaster himself.

(c) Novice parachutists must:

1. Initially make five (5) static sport parachute jumps;

2. Successfully pull a dummy ripcord on three (3) successive static line jumps without loss of stability or control.

(d) Maximum ground winds for novice parachutists: 10 m.p.h.

100.23 Minimum Opening Altitudes

Minimum pack opening altitudes above the ground for parachutists shall be:

(a) Student and novice parachutists: 2,500 ft. above the ground.

(b) Class A and B License holders: 2,500 ft. above the ground.

(c) Class C License holders: 2,000 ft. above the ground.

(d) Class D License holders: 2,000 ft. above the ground.

100.25 Drop Zone Requirements

(a) All areas used for parachuting must be unobstructed, with the following minimum radial distances to the nearest hazard:

1. Student and novice parachutists: 300 meters.

2. Class A and B License holders: 200 meters.

3. Class C License holders: 100 meters.

4. Class D License holders: unlimited.

NOTE: Hazards are defined as: trees, ditches, telephone and power lines, towers, buildings, highways, and automobiles.

(b) Manned ground-to-air communications (e.g., radios, panels, smoke, lights) must be present on the drop zone during parachuting operations.

100.27 Pre-Jump Requirements

The appropriate altitude and surface winds will be determined prior to conducting any parachute jump.

100.29 Extraordinary Parachute Jumps

(a) Night, water, and exhibition parachute jumps may be performed only with the approval of the local USPA Area Safety Office (ASO) or USPA Instructor/Examiner.

(b) Pre-planned breakaway jumps may be made only by Class C and Class D License holders using FAA TSO'ed equipment.

(c) Batwings are prohibited. ("Batwings" are defined as any jumpsuit extensions that extend past the elbow or extend past the waist or below the knees or have any rigid or semi-rigid parts or any other device that may restrict the arm or leg movements of the jumper in freefall.)

SUBPART D—EQUIPMENT

100.31 Parachutists' Equipment

Each parachutist must be equipped with:

(a) Flotation gear when the intended exit point, opening point or landing point of a parachutist is within one mile of an open body of water (an open body of water is defined as one in which a parachutist could drown);

(b) A light when performing night jumps; and

(c) For student and novice parachutists, a rigid or HALO helmet.

100.41 Special Altitude Equipment, Supplementary Oxygen.

Supplementary oxygen is mandatory on parachute jumps performed over 15,000 feet (MSL).

CHAPTER V
BEYOND THE STATIC LINE
YOUR FREEFALL PROGRESSION

After your first jump, your introduction to sport parachuting, you will make some more static line jumps, a minimum of five, before being signed off for freefall. In some countries they require 20 or 30 rope jumps to be assured you will pull on freefall but in North America we have always required just five. The smaller number has not only proven sufficient, it is less apt to discourage the novice who is anxious to progress. On your static line jumps, you will be making dummy ripcord pulls (DRCP). If your jumps are perfect, you get the handle out "by the numbers" and without losing stability or control on jumps 3, 4, and 5, you will next be permitted to "do-it-yourself."

There is very little air time during your initial training, especially on static line and short delays so you will only have time to perform your planned maneuver once. In fact, the jump is more of a test than a learning experience so a lot of thought and practice on the ground are required. Use the training aids, think about what you plan to do on this jump and make dry runs over and over. With this approach you will progress faster because you are making fewer mistakes in the air. This will provide you with a greater sense of accomplishment and you will have more fun. It is always nice to do well especially in an exciting new challenge such as sport parachuting.

Your last static line jump and your first freefall will be on the same day, so plan your weekend considering the number of jumps you plan to make each day. Most students make two and three is the limit. Sport parachuting requires a lot of ground preparation and is quite tiring so, unless you are jumping at a commercial center where they take care of the carrying and packing of the gear, you will probably find that three jumps take all day and wear you out. The experienced jumpers may make a dozen jumps in a day while doing their own packing but most call it a day after five.

Your first one off the "dope rope" will be a jump and pull. It will go just like your static line DRCP jumps except that this is one of your great parachuting milestones. You are on your own, you did it yourself and you feel great.

Assuming that you have been devoting a lot of time to your ground practice and your jumpmaster liked your jump and pull, it is time to graduate to five second delays and start learning freefall. You will be making a minimum of three each of 5, 10, 15 and 20 second delays and will progress from each to the next as soon as your jumpmaster is convinced you

---

"Just as planning prepares you mentally, ground practise helps your body get used to going through the motions" — George Wright.

are ready. At each level, you will have certain skills to master. During your first 30 jumps or so you will have good days and some not so satisfying. While you enjoy a sense of accomplishment, these jumps are more work than fun. In fact, if you drop out prior to amassing 1,000 jumps and qualifying for your gold wings, it will most likely be at this time.

On fives you will be concentrating on your count, on pulling on the fifth second after exit. This is a time to polish your pull and work on your canopy control.

On tens, you will become conscious of wind, noise and speed while you learn the frog position, start your turns and begin using instruments. The needle of the altimeter doesn't move much on a ten so you will have to concentrate on a watch and back it up with your count. When you are on twenties, you will switch to the usual altimeter and unless you put some tape over the watch for a jump or two, you will probably not see the altimeter at all; your eye will automatically concentrate on the watch each time you look down.

On fifteens, you are into real skydiving, the world of "terminal velocity". This is the greatest speed at which you can fall through the air. The resistance to the air (your size) overcomes the pull of gravity (your weight) until they balance out at about the 12th second after exit. In the spread, stable face to earth position this will be about 54 mps (120 mph). This speed provides more control than you had on your subterminal jumps so you will find your maneuvers to be surer and quicker. On fifteens, you fall quite a way prior to pull and your jumpmaster may not be able to follow all of your airwork so he may elect to exit after you for a closer view. You will be spotting by now, if you weren't working on it from the beginning, and your turns should be getting better. You will be more relaxed in the frog position and won't be buffeting; you'll be in control.

On twenties, you will polish up your 360 degree turns, try the delta position and experiment with tracking. You will start reading your altimeter and this is most appropriate because your rate of descent increases greatly in a head down position.

You will stay on thirties until you have logged at least 20 stable freefalls, can make figure eights (two alternate 360 degree turns) and have demonstrated your spotting and canopy control by landing within 50 meters of the target center on five delays of 20 seconds or more.

All of your jumps will be made under the direct supervision of a USPA rated jumpmaster until your instructor is satisfied that you can take care of yourself and signs you off as being "off instruction". This isn't the end of your learning, just the end of your direct supervision. Once you have been certified as capable of jumpmastering yourself, you will be allowed to board the jumpship without a jumpmaster in tow and may even jump from a small two place plane carrying just you and the pilot.

Now is the time to start thinking about taking the written exam for the Class A license. The other requirements are as follows:

    a. Completed 25 freefall parachute jumps including:

       1. 12 controlled delays of at least 10 seconds.

       2. 6 controlled delays of at least 20 seconds.

       3. 3 controlled delays of at least 30 seconds.

       4. 10 freefall jumps landing within 50 meters of target center during which the novice selected the exit and opening points.

    b. Demonstrated ability to hold heading during freefall and make 360 degree flat turns to both the right and left.

    c. Demonstrated ability to safety jumpmaster himself, to include independently selecting the proper altitude and properly using correct exit and opening points.

    d. Demonstrated ability to properly pack his own main parachute and conduct safety checks on his and other parachutist's equipment prior to a jump.

    e. A logbook endorsement by a USPA Instructor/Examiner, a USPA Instructor, his CSO or ASO that he has received training for unintentional water landings.

    f. Passed a written examination conducted by a USPA Instructor/Examiner, USPA Instructor, his CSO or ASO.

> *"Any deviation from the horizontal plane is just plain poison for most people. Everybody likes to go fast and do things but, for some obscure reason, their ingrained fear of doing it straight down still persists."*

The A license is analogous to a Private Pilot license or a driver's license, you aren't a novice anymore. It is another great milestone in your parachuting career and a time to celebrate. You will be making door exits and going higher to 45's and 60's. Your relative work jumping will become more and more exciting as the number of people in the air with you increases. This is where the fun really begins in parachuting; this is what makes the first 30 jumps worth it. Now let's get down to the specifics of basic freefall.

RIPCORD PULLS

You will probably become more sensitive to the pull time as you progress up the delay ladder. During your static lines and early delays, you will leave the step in a poised exit almost standing head up. Later as you approach terminal velocity (after 12 seconds), your head will drop more until you are parallel with the ground and your air work will become more important than your exit. Now for the first time you will have the time and air resistance to make corrections. Stability, especially in pitch (head up-down), will be much more noticeable. If you go head down on the pull, you will probably find it terribly unnerving and on the next jump you won't be looking forward to this part of it. And, you may find yourself counting down and making a quick grab for the handle in order to avoid going head down. There are easier, more satisfactory ways to combat the problem.

There are two ways to go through the pull you might like to consider. The first, just as you did on your DRCP jumps, bring both arms in to the main lift webs by bending the elbows and reversing the palms so they face the chest. This will place your right hand on the handle while the left arm mirrors the right so you won't lose roll (shoulder/hip up-down) stability. If you can think to bend the legs at the knees a little more at the same time, you won't go head down and the pull will be a very satisfying one. The second approach to pulling involves bringing the left hand over the head while reaching in with the right for the ripcord handle. This method not only counteracts the tendency to go head down, it will provide you with any corrections in the other axes (turns and rolls) you may require.

Years ago, before jumpers were converting their military surplus harnesses to the right hand outboard pull, many students were taught to make two-handed pulls from the center of their chest. Today however, the two-handed pull is usually reserved for the "hard pull" situations.

Some students have trouble locating the main ripcord. Every piece of rental or club gear is adjusted a little differently; you can't expect the handle to be in exactly the same place every time. It is, therefore, essential that you look for the handle prior to reaching for it. The technique is to push the head back (to help you arch) while bringing the chin down to the chest and lowering the eyes to visually locate the handle. Look at the ripcord and you won't miss it with your hand.

Soon you will be waving your hands by crossing your arms over your head. This is a "wave-off" which you are practising for use on your relative jumps. It is a signal to those above you that you are about to pull.

USING INSTRUMENTS

You will use one or more of the four basic ways to keep track of your time, distance and position: verbal count, stopwatch, altimeter and eyeballing it. The count is used initially because the watch and altimeter are not practical on short delays; they just don't move much. You will count by thousands, "one-thousand, two-thousand, three-thousand," etc., to space your drill to avoid the natural tendency to race through it. If you count too fast, you won't delay the full five or ten seconds and you may not have enough time to practice your air work. Then too, your jumpmaster may not graduate you to the next higher level because you have yet to master this one. You started by counting actions, not numbers when you shouted "arch-thousand, reach-thousand, etc". Later you will just count numbers but after the pull you will still count off the emergency procedure always anticipating a total malfunction.

Altimeters and watches are mechanical and though they may be relied upon most of the time, they are subject to failure. The watch must be punched on exit and it doesn't always start so learn to "eyeball" the terrain, learn what 750 meters (2500') looks like so you'll recognize it the next time you encounter it.

FREEFALL TABLES

Distances fallen are calculated for freefall in a stable spread position with average temperature and pressure conditions for a sea level drop zone. Also see the Conversion Table in Chapter II.

Distance Fallen Each Second to Terminal Velocity				
Seconds From Exit	Meters per Second	Feet Per Second	KMS Per Hour	Miles Per Hour
1	4.8	16	17.5	10.91
2	14	46	50.4	31.36
3	23	76	83.3	51.81
4	31.5	104	114.0	70.91
5	38	124	136.0	84.54
6	42.5	138	151.4	94.09
7	45	148	162.4	100.91
8	47.5	156	171.1	106.36
9	49.5	163	178.8	111.14
10	51	167	183.2	113.86
11	52	171	187.6	116.59
12	53.5	176	190.9	118.64
each additional second	53.5	176	190.9	118.64

General Rule:
After terminal velocity is reached (about 12 seconds), it takes 5.7 seconds to free fall each 1000 feet.

CUMULATIVE DISTANCE FALLEN IN FREE FALL SPREAD POSITION

Second of free fall	Meters	Feet	Second of free fall	Meters	Feet
1	4.8	16	15	612.5	2010
2	19	62	20	884	2900
3	42	138	25	1150	3770
4	74	242	30	1415	4650
5	111.5	366	35	1685	5530
6	153.5	504	40	1955	6410
7	198.7	652	45	2220	7290
8	246.5	808	50	2490	8170
9	295.5	970	55	2760	9050
10	347.5	1140	60	3025	9930
11	399.5	1310	65	3295	10810
12	452.5	1485	70	3565	11690
13	506	1660	75	3830	12570
14	561	1840			

RECOMMENDED EXIT ALTITUDES FOR PACK OPENING OF 2500' ABOVE DROP ZONE

Type of jump	Feet Above DZ	Meters
Static line	2800	850
Clear & Pull	3000	915
5 sec delay	3000	915
7	3280	1000
10	3600	1100
15	4500	1370
20	5400	1645
25	6300	1920
27	6550	1995
30	7200	2200
40	8900	2710
45	9800	2990
50	10700	3260
55	11600	3535
60	12400	3780
64	13100	3995
75	15100	4600

CAUTION, The rate of descent increases with (1) other body positions, (2) higher temperatures, (3) lower pressure (e.g. higher field elevation). Use this table with extreme caution at field elevations over 1000 feet, especially during long delays. The newer, oversize jumpsuits *slow* descent.

STABILITY AND BODY POSITIONS

"Stability" is a balance of forces. It occurs where you are falling in a selected position (e.g. face to earth) without requiring constant correcting movements. You are relaxed, at ease and not rotating on any axes. Because of the distribution of your body and parachute weight, it is impossible to freefall in a standing position so we must select another

"When the people look like ants – PULL, when the ants look like people – PRAY".

acceptable comfortable alternative such as lying face down. This position is familiar, allows a good field of view and gives you the feeling of flying like Superman. The only other positions you could maintain are back to earth and the head to earth "delta" and, obviously, they aren't as satisfying as the face to earth position. Now, using your arms and legs as control surfaces, you can do most anything an airplane can do but go back up.

Since we are trying to learn stability, it should be mentioned that it is possible to become unstable or "Z" (out of control). Buffeting (oscillating about one axis such as pitch; head up-down) can be corrected by relaxing and moving the arms or legs just a bit. It doesn't happen often and may not occur until you have several jumps so the greatest problem may be in recognizing it until after the jump is over. Uncontrolled turns, slow or fast are caused by unequal alignment of the legs, arms and/or trunk. Most students have no idea what their legs are doing because they can't see them; they must be in identical positions. If you go unstable at altitude, go ahead and correct it. If you are unstable at pull time, pull anyway. It is better to be stable during unpacking but it is best to be unpacking regardless of position. At opening altitude, you are running out of time fast. Even if poor body position causes a malfunction, you're still slowed to about a tenth of your freefall rate of descent, so you have plenty of time to think about proper emergency procedures.

THE FROG POSITION

The frog position

The "frog" is a relaxed, modified stable face to earth freefall position without an arch, with the legs bent and the arms in a "U". It is the common advanced flying position from which you will make all maneuvers. To practice the frog, start from the basic spread and then gradually relax it by bending the arms at the elbows and legs at the knees. Feel your way into it and make mirror image limb movements so as to maintain stability. You won't be able to watch your legs but you can keep the hands in view out of the corners of your eyes. If you relax at terminal velocity, your body will naturally flow into the frog position.

The frog may be further modified by tightening it. Your reduced drag will cause you to increase your rate of descent without going head down into a delta position. The frog is tightened simply by pulling in the arms and legs. The opposite, called the "spider" is used to slow the descent and is accomplished by spreading out as far as possible and reversing the arch as though you were on top of a large rubber ball. The frog, tight and regular, and the spider are common relative work positions. They allow you to alter your descent speed relative to other freefalling jumpers without creating unwanted horizontal movement. In the tight frog, control becomes more difficult; the "balancing" is done by hand movements from the wrist. You can expect this to take a few jumps to find and perfect.

"At pull time, you pull – regardless of body position" — Mike Truffer

THE BACK TO EARTH STABLE POSITION

The back to earth or "rocking chair" position. Note the reversed arch.

If you bend at the waist, you'll fall back to earth.

The stable back to earth position isn't terribly useful except as a training maneuver. Getting over, holding it and getting back will provide you with the confidence that if you ever do find yourself out of visual contact with the ground, you can correct the situation. The easiest way to get over is with a barrel roll (discussed later in this chapter) and it is easy to maintain with a reverse arch. Now you'll be able to see both your hands and feet at work. To return to the face-to-earth position you can arch hard but this takes some time. You might do half a forward loop or half a back loop but you must master the loops first. The simplest way is to return with another barrel roll. While over on your back, do not trust your altimeter, especially if it is chest mounted. It is in a partial vacuum area and will not indicate accurately.

THE DELTA POSITION

The delta position. The arms and legs may be spread for increased control.

The delta is a stable fall position with the head down providing a much increased descent rate. It is normally used in relative work to descend down to the action. The arms are swept back and maneuvering is done with the shoulders, hands and/or legs. The arms may be spread or tight against the sides and the legs may be spread or pressed together.

Altitude and speed are two things to watch in the delta. You may accelerate from 54 meters/second in the face to earth position to some 80 meters/second and this speed plus the head to earth body position will make your opening something to remember. So, flare out to a stable spread position and slow down before dumping your main. Since you are eating up the altitude so much faster, you'll want to keep an eye on the altimeter. A good, tight delta is a lot of fun; you can feel the great increase in speed as the air tears at your jumpsuit.

AERIAL MANEUVERS,
vertical/horizontal flight and aerobatics

With simple movements of body surfaces the freefalling parachutist may increase and decrease his vertical speed, cover a significant amount of ground horizontally and perform every aerobatic maneuver as though suspended by invisible threads. This is true flying, the closest you will ever come to imitating the birds without large cumbersome wing-like equipment.

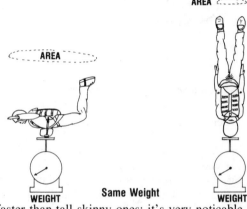

Your attitude does not change your weight but it does affect your drag and resulting air speed. As you alter your profile to the relative wind, you alter your air resistance (drag).

WEIGHT   Same Weight   WEIGHT

Short fat people freefall at terminal faster than tall skinny ones; it's very noticable in relative work. Your speed in freefall is determined by your weight and your air resistance (drag). If you wish to fall faster, you must increase weight or decrease drag. Conversely, if you wish to fall slower, you must lose weight or get bigger in area. Relative work is flying and doing so in relation to other fliers. In freefall it isn't practical to add and shed weight so you are left with changing your drag area. Fortunately this is rather easy; by simply standing on your head, you can increase your vertical speed by as much as 50% (54-80 mps).

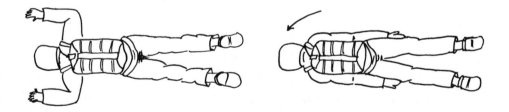

Arms up — body level   **Arms back — head down**

"The air! Man has visions of flight – not the roaring progress of heavy sinking machines, but that silent loveliness of gliding on outstretched arms that comes to everyone in dreams" — Frank S. Stuart, *City of the Bees*.

In the spread stable face to earth position or the frog, your body's weight is concentrated in the center and your limbs are both vanes and control surfaces, very much like an airplane. You are balanced with an equal amount of air resistance on the limbs all around the weight in the center. Now, if you move your hands and arms rearward, reducing the supporting drag on the upper part of your body, you will go into a head down attitude. Or, if you put your hands straight up over your head and draw your knees up to your chest, you will start into a backloop. You can even turn (yaw axis) by simply dropping a shoulder as this places a twist in the body so that it takes on a shape somewhat like a propeller. So by altering your flying surfaces, you can perform most any aerobatic maneuver.

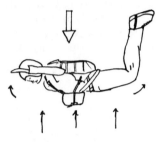

Level: the air flows around the body evenly.

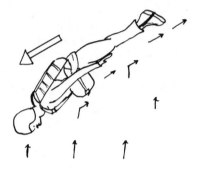

At an angle: the air is deflected around the body producing horizontal motion.

When you are freefalling in a face to earth position such as the frog, your body plows through the air forcing it to flow evenly all around you. But when you angle your body, such as in a delta, the air is deflected and this imparts some horizontal movement; your body acts like a sled.

So, it can be seen that all your aerial maneuvers are initiated and achieved through the alteration of your control surfaces (hands, legs, etc.) which change the attitude of your body varying its effective surface area with respect to the relative wind, shifts your center of gravity or causes a deflection in the air flowing past your body.

Once again, ground practice and review will increase your chances of success in the air. It helps to know what you are doing before you go up. If your DZ does not have a horizontal hammock-like training device, a lot of these maneuvers may be practiced on a small table or even a bar stool.

TRACKING

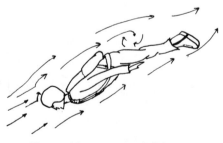

The track is a modified delta, a position used to cover ground. It is even more effective with tandem back mounted parachutes.

"All motion is relative to the observer" – Albert Einstein.

The track position is most often used by the parachutist who discovers he has erred in spotting or drifted in freefall and uses it to get back to the opening point. Even more important, it is used to "turn and track" when jumpers separate after relative work and before opening. The track is a further refined delta which forms the body into a rough airfoil like the profile of an airplane's wing. This position is designed to produce some lift in addition to the force of the deflected air to move the body through the air horizontally. It has been theorized that in a "max track", one can achieve an angle of 35 degrees or more from the vertical, or approaching 1:1. This means that on a sixty second delay from 12,500' providing 10,000' (3,000m) of track time, one could cover 7,000' (2,100m) of ground, that's 1.35 miles!

To learn the track position, start with a delta to build up some working speed. Then bend slightly at the waist, roll your shoulders forward, bend your arms to follow the body, cup your hands, force your head back, straighten your legs positioning them about shoulder width apart and point your toes. You should be able to feel and see the difference but, remember, it takes time to build up speed so get into position and hold it for a while. When your really starting to develop lift, you'll feel your dive flatten out quite a bit. The track can be steered by gently guiding with your arms, hands, shoulders or head.

The track, like the delta, involves a much higher terminal velocity so remember to flare for several seconds before you dump your main. The track is not only fun, it is one of the most important positions. It should not only be tried, it must be mastered.

TURNS

Turns are a movement about the vertical (yaw) axis and are the most important of your basic maneuvers.

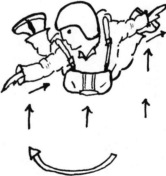

Even minor tilting of the palms will cause a turn.   **To turn, twist your body like a propeller.**

When you are 12 seconds out and falling at terminal, you have a lot of relative wind to work with, a lot of air to push on. From the frog position, even angling both hands 45 degrees the same direction will produce a slow turn. Study it on your next drive to the DZ by sticking your hand out the window of the car. At 95 kph (just under 60 mph) you are doing only half the speed of face to earth freefall; there is far more pressure up there.

There are many ways to effect a turn, in fact, the trick is in *not* turning. Any alteration in the position of your hands, arms, legs, body, etc., will produce a turn unless counteracted by another body part. Some of these specialized turns such as the "push turn" are used for certain types of jumps such as style competition.

"If you can start a turn, you can stop a spin" — Ted Strong.

In turning, the twist is the trick. Turns are made in the same way from the frog, delta or track positions; just lower a shoulder. In the frog position, the hands and arms help too.

To learn ''natural'' turns, exit the aircraft, assume the frog position and build up speed to near terminal; they'll be sluggish if you start right off the step. Bring your hands back just a bit so you are very slightly head low then look in the direction you wish to go. Bend your head that direction and dip that hand and shoulder. Your body will follow your eyes. Soon, turns will become second nature, automatic. Like riding a bicycle or swimming, you won't have to deliberate over every movement. In time, even stability will become automatic. When reaching out for another jumper in the air, your leg will compensate subconsciously, you won't even know it. To stop the turning, just straighten back to your frog position. If you are turning fast, you may have to position yourself for a turn in the opposite direction so as not to overshoot your heading.

There are a few more important points worth remembering. Turns are not immediate; it takes time to build up speed. So hold the position until it takes effect and then be prepared to stop your turn just before you come around to your heading. Use a ground reference point for a heading and make it something that will be easy to find when you come around. Remember that subterminal turns are slow and mushy, unlike the turns you will find after 12 seconds out. If you should get into trouble practicing turns and can't stop one with an opposite correcting turn, assume the delta position. Once straightened out, go back into the frog. You can always delta out of a spin. But remember to keep track of your altitude and pull at pull time whether you're stable or not.

Two 360 degree turns in opposite directions are combined and called a ''figure eight''. Mastery of this maneuver is one of the requirements for the ''A'' licence.

THE BARREL ROLL

The barrel roll should be your first aerobatic maneuver because it is easy, not as potentially frightening as a loop, will help you practice SDB (Stable Delay Back to earth) and mastery of it is good insurance in case you ever find yourself on your back unexpectedly.

The barrel roll.

To make a barrel roll from the frog position, straighten your legs and pull them almost together while sticking your arms straight out to the side. Then bring one arm in across the chest while dipping (rolling) that shoulder. The sudden loss of drag on that side of your body will cause it to drop and roll you onto your back. To complete the roll, extend the folded arm and bring in the other one. Then resume the spread arm position as soon as the ground comes into view again. Do it again with more coordination and it will be smoother. Once you feel confident about it, try it from the frog position and accelerate it by throwing your arm and shoulder under and into it. Because your arms are in, you will do the complete roll in an instant.

First forward loop.　　　　　　　　**Improved forward loop.**

Forward loops are easy though, at first, going head down may make you a bit anxious. Just as we did with the barrel roll, we will start with a "safe" method and then we'll clean it up into an improved loop.

Extend your legs straight back and spread them just slightly. Then put your arms straight out assuming a "T" position. This will give you lateral stability so you won't fall off to one side. Now simply bend way forward at the waist. The sudden loss of drag on the upper part of your body will cause your head to drop and you will go all the way around. When the ground comes into view again, straighten your body. You may wish to throw the arms high in a flare to stop on the level. Once you feel confident about these elementary forward loops, try them from a frog position by bending at the waist and throwing yourself into it. You should be able to perform two of them with ease on a twenty even if you wait to begin until you are near terminal velocity, 12 seconds from exit. If you find yourself on your back having completed only half a loop, you may wish to use a barrel roll to get back over.

THE BACK LOOP

Improved backloop.

First backloop.

The backloop is just like doing a gainer into a swimming pool but you don't have to worry about hitting the diving board. First the safe method and then the improved loop.

Extend the legs straight back, spread just slightly. Then put your arms straight out assuming a "T" position. This will provide you with lateral stability so you won't fall off to the side. Now quickly bring the knees up to the chest. The sudden loss of drag on the lower part of your body will cause it to drop and you should go all the way over. When the ground comes into view again, straighten the body and flare. Once you feel confident about this elementary method, try the backloop from the frog position. Simultaneously push forward and down with your arms as you pull the knees to the chest and throw back the head. The momentum should carry you all the way over. Flare when the ground comes into view again.

A sloppy or incomplete backloop may leave you on your back. A barrel roll is probably the easiest and fastest way to return to the familiar face to earth position should this happen.

OTHER POSITIONS AND MANEUVERS

There are other freefall positions and maneuvers such as the style tuck, hand track, backslide, knee turn and so on which you will want to attempt after mastering the above mentioned basics. Once you can handle the above, all others will be easy.

DOOR EXITS

The unpoised, door exit is a prerequisite to relative work.

Door exits are a thrill. They are one of parachuting's training milestones and provide you with a great feeling of accomplishment. The satisfaction you will feel is equivalent to your first freefall, your first sighting of another jumper in the air, etc. You must master the door exit as it is the last of the basic skills required for beginning relative work and "RW" is what jumping is all about.

Now that you feel confident about your loops and rolls, you know you can recover if you should suddenly find yourself on your back so there is no reason to be apprehensive about an unpoised exit. There is no need to exit the aircraft face to earth or even stable as long as you are in complete, continual control.

Let's start with a warmup jump; a modified poised exit. Get in the door and when you are ready to go, reach for the strut with your left hand, put your left foot on the step and then just swing out and go. As you leave the step, your position is just like the old poised, stable one but your right hand and right foot never made contact with the plane. This one looks good and is a great confidence builder.

Now a real door exit, straight out perpendicular to the fuselage. Just dive out with your arms swept back, do a forward loop and flare. Nothing to it and it happens so fast! You might get flipped by the prop blast and relative wind but it isn't likely because your profile is very small. The exit goes quickly and you are out of the prop blast and going much slower by the time you flareout face to earth.

Next, try the same exit without the front loop. Once you clear the door, arch, throw your hands high and bring your feet together to counteract the loop. (This looks like a Superman swoop). Try some straight out and try some with turns into the direction of flight. Make corrections by adjusting your body position and avoid kicking or attempting corrections by throwing your body around. You'll love door exits and will never go back to the poised type except for some specialized hanging-on type group exits.

93

To practice for RW and be ready to learn big formation work, try exiting head first and transitioning smoothly from the Superman swoop into a tight delta. Gradually move the hands and arms down close to the body and spread your legs about shoulder width. It will take several jumps to get the feel of it but you will use it a lot later.

There are many things to do in the short time you have in freefall, so don't spend all of it on the exit. After leaving the aircraft, get on with your other airwork, canopy work, etc.

RELATIVE WORK

Relative work is the intentional maneuvering of two or more parachutists in close proximity to one another during freefall. Fast-moving precision freefall relative work is the most rapidly growing aspect of sport parachuting today. It's fun, fast and exciting; there is something to learn and enjoy on every jump. RW is an activity that requires teamwork; it is a coordinated balancing act requiring maximum effort from each and every participant. The preparation is great while the time is short and anyone in the air can blow the jump by taking out the fragile formation. When successful, it is an incomparable joy to be shared by all. Whereas relative jumping was once a "hit or miss" affair between two jumpers, it is now an exact aerodynamic science often involving 30 or more participants.

RW was born in the U.S. in 1958 when Steve Snyder and Charlie Hillard made the first baton pass. In subsequent years, the stick was abandoned but small "star" formations were being accomplished routinely. Size was usually held to four, the capacity of most jump planes. In 1965 at Taft, California, the "Arvin Good Guys" put the first 8-man together. Taft was also the site of the first ten-man in 1967 and the Center even hosted a ten-man competition later the same year. Credential type recognition also began that year when Bill Newell established the Star Crest and began issuing patches to those who had been in stars of eight or larger. In 1970, a four-man RW event was added to the National Championships; it wasn't "large star" but it was "RW". Ted Webster led an RW team to the 1970 World Championships in Bled, Yugoslavia, to make demonstration jumps and this turned on the world! A ten-man speed star event was introduced at the 1972 U.S. Nationals; interest in large star RW was booming. The Commission Internationale de Parachutisme accepted RW in 1973 and both 4-man and ten-man were now world wide events. Interest soared! Equipment changed, big planes were located, jumpers drove great distances to get together to jump the big birds. Everyone was doing RW. Novices aspired to it and old timers learned

> *"The exultation of seeing fine relative work flying is surpassed only by the joy of being part of the jump yourself"* — Pat Works

something new; RW put the fun back into jumping. At the end of 1976 in Zephyrhills, Florida, over 100 ten-man teams entered the annual meet. Through 1975 and '76, the large star interest turned to sequential RW, the plain old star was passé. Now they were doing snowflakes and accordians, donuts and even flying back to earth. The CIP met again in 1977 and adopted the eight-man sequential event for world competition. Then jumpers began doing the ''impossible'', zipping around formations crossing over other bodies intentionally and using the drop in the burble to position themselves. They made three dimensional formations with one or more standing up! It was incredible. RW is obviously limited only by the imagination.

You will be eligible to begin your relative training once you have your ''A'' License, are able to perform all the elementary maneuvers mentioned previously including door exits and have logged ten minutes of freefall time. It is essential that you have a thorough understanding of RW and it is highly recommended that you pick up a copy of THE ART OF FREEFALL RELATIVE WORK by Pat Works. It is available through all parachute dealers or direct from the author for $7.45 (1656-P Beechwood Avenue, Fullerton, CA 92635). Jamey Woodward has published a training outline on RW for the USPA. This syllabus and USPA Part 117 ''Relative Work Doctrine'' should be available from your instructor or you may write the USPA direct.

Pre-jump planning is even more important in RW than in solo leaps. When you are on your own, lousy flying hurts only you. In a group, mistakes may take out the formation or even cause injuries and this is no way to make friends. So it pays to talk to anyone you can and read everything you can find. Get the publications mentioned above and educate yourself. You'll save time and friendships.

Your initial RW training will probably be with your instructor, one-on-one. He will help you with the basics. Your first hookup will be followed with practice in vertical/horizontal maneuvers, exits/dives, the approach, docking, the breakoff, etc.

If you find trouble getting on the loads with the big guys it's only because you're a turkey and not yet ready to soar with the eagles. Remember that the other jumpers have a lot riding on the jump; they have invested a great deal of time and money and they want a successful formation. They dislike being targets for the less experienced and have a right to be selective.

You would probably only make a mistake anyway, so develop your own skill working in small groups, beginning with twos. The best RW practice may be performed with just two participants. Get together with another big load reject and polish the basics. Once you are making hoopups consistently, switch the exit order. Is the linkup smooth? Can you do it subterminal? Six seconds out the door? Can you fly side by side without touching? When you are good enough, when you have tried hard enough, the eagles will notice. Then you'll have to remember to be kind to turkeys.

It is not the purpose of this elementary text to attempt a detailed discussion of the advanced stages of the sport. This information is available elsewhere, as noted, so there is no value in repeating it here.

SPOTTING

''Spotting'' is the selection of the course to fly on jump run, directing the pilot on that course and deciding on the correct point on the ground over which to leave the aircraft in order to land in the target area. There is more to it than just looking down for the ''spot'' as it

---

''Relative work puts the fun, comradeship and the excitement back into the sport'' — Ned Luker

There is more to spotting than simply looking straight down.

depends upon the wind and several other factors.

Accurate spotting requires the ascertainment of the opening point and the exit point. On low jumps, these will be virtually the same but on high ones, there are many factors to consider.

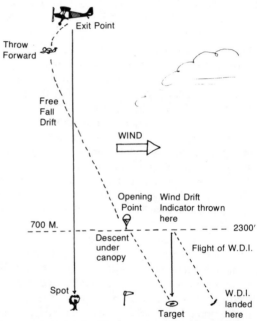

Exit Point

Throw Forward

Free Fall Drift

WIND

Opening Point

Wind Drift Indicator thrown here

700 M. — — — — — — — — — — — — 2300′

Descent under canopy

Flight of W.D.I.

A side view of "spotting" or selecting the exit point.

Spot

Target

W.D.I. landed here

To begin with, let's think of the total descent as being in three separate phases: the 'throw forward', the 'freefall drift' and the canopy ride. As you exit, you are traveling the same speed as the jump plane and are thrown forward across the ground. Your trajectory is dependent mostly upon the speed of the aircraft at time of exit. The freefall drift is that distance you are moved by the upper winds (those between the aircraft and the canopy deployment) and the third segment consists of the slower two minutes you spend descending under your canopy to the target area.

So, we must locate and consider four important points: the landing point (target), opening point (by compensating for ground winds), exit point (by compensating for the winds aloft and forward throw) and the engine cut point (to allow the plane to slow down and to compensate for the exit lag).

"Many of the people asking to get on ten-man loads aren't capable of making consistent two-mans!" — Bob Iverson

---

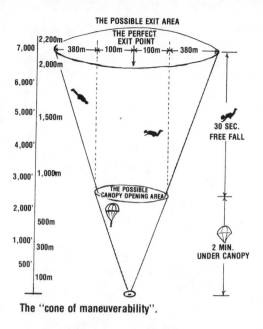

THE POSSIBLE EXIT AREA

THE PERFECT EXIT POINT

2,200m ← 380m → ← 100m → ← 100m → ← 380m →

7,000'
2,000m
6,000'
5,000' 1,500m
4,000'
30 SEC. FREE FALL
3,000' 1,000m
THE POSSIBLE CANOPY OPENING AREA
2,000'
500m
1,000' 300m
2 MIN. UNDER CANOPY
500'
100m

The "cone of maneuverability".

Both tracking and canopy speed will make up for bad spotting to some extent.

The streamer run.
A. Direct aircraft over target center,
B. Throw wind drift indicator directly over target and punch stop watch.
C. Pilot makes shallow turns to the right keeping streamer in view through jump door.
D. Streamer lands, punch stop watch again.

Because both you and your canopy have a horizontal movement capability, you can make up for an imperfect spot to some degree as well as compensate for changing conditions. The ever decreasing safety margin is called the "cone of maneuverability" and you must stay inside it. If you stray just one meter outside, there is no way you can get any closer to the disc than one meter unless the wind changes. As you descend, the area becomes smaller and the situation more critical. Stay inside and you always have a chance at the disc.

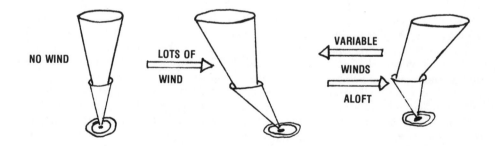

NO WIND

LOTS OF WIND

VARIABLE WINDS ALOFT

Now, crank in some wind and the cones take on their real shape.

You should always spot as though you were jumping an unmodified canopy and aim for the very center, the perfect exit point. This will allow you maximum compensation for errors and may be a blessing to the guy on your load who has to use his unmodified reserve.

First, locate the landing point, presumably this is the disc in the center of the landing area.

There are two practical ways to measure the wind for determining the opening point. Some of the larger centers use a balloon system. They release a balloon and track it with a theodolite and note its azimuth in time increments. Knowing the rate of ascent and consulting a chart, they can plot the opening point on a premarked aerial map for all to see. The second is by dropping a wind drift indicator over the target at opening altitude. The WDI is normally a weighted piece of crepe paper designed to descend at the same rate as an open canopy. The wind will differ in intensity and direction at different levels and the specifics are nice to know when shooting an accuracy jump. Otherwise, it is sufficient to pick a point from the streamer drop and accept the mean effect of the wind.

AIRBORNE PARALLELOGRAM

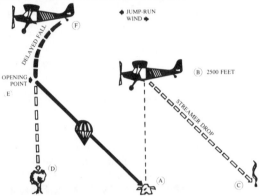

On the first pass, drop the wind drift indicator over the target (A) at opening altitude (B). Draw an imaginary line from its landing point (C) through the target (A) to a point an equal distance upwind (D). This becomes the ground reference for the opening point (E) and the exit point (F).

Throwing the wind drift indicator.

Before takeoff, the pilot will select an approximate wind line based on his best guess in assessing the direction of the ground winds. Ordinarily, he will fly the streamer drop by approaching the target directly into the wind to minimize ground speed and give you as much time as possible. This will also minimize side drift; it's hard to spot when the aircraft is not moving and pointing in the same direction. Make sure you have at least two WDI's aboard, keep one in reserve. Unroll the streamer a short distance and bunch it up and don't grip it tightly with a sweaty hand; you want it to unwind when you release it. Give course corrections to the pilot by direction and then amount, such as "right — five" and wait a few seconds before spotting again so that the plane can level back out. If the pilot is on the radio or otherwise occupied, use hand signals. Throw the streamer down and back forcefully so as to miss both the step and the tail, then punch your stop watch.

Make sure the wind drift indicator has unrolled properly and keep your eyes on it. If the pilot is not skilled at flying jumpers, suggest that he keep an eye on it. This way he will make climbing circles with the wing not too low and you will be able to see it too. If you take your eyes off the streamer, it is sure to disappear against nature's camouflage, especially toward the end of the drop. The timing should reveal about one minute per thousand feet. If it wasn't, you will want to compensate on the length of the spot.

Eyeball the WDI on the ground, then the target and then an equal distance upwind of the target. This is the opening point and you have built your "airborne parallelogram". Always take advantage of all the wind speed and direction indicators available to you rather than relying solely on the WDI. If the last lift is making the target, how does their spot compare

---

"Good judgement comes from experience, and experience – well, that comes from poor judgement"

98

with the direction indicated by the wind sock? When the smoke leaves that chimney, does it change course after rising a bit? At what angle does it leave the stack? Which way are those small puffy clouds moving? Check the shadows on the ground. Is anyone down there kicking up dust? Look for farm machinery, cars on dirt roads, etc.

The opening point will be up wind from the target about .4 km for each 8 kph of wind velocity (¼ mile for each 5mph.) In fact, it may be more since the wind usually blows faster as you go higher due to the friction provided by the ground. The distance adds up fast.

There are other complications too. Heat waves create a mirage and makes the target appear to be further down wind than it is. It is only about 5 meters for each knot of ground wind but this will make a difference if there is a dog leg in the wind, i.e. the ground and upper winds are up to 90 degrees different.

The next consideration is the selection of the exit point so that you will reach the opening point when it's time to dump. For low jumps, the exit and opening points will be the same but there is quite a difference on longer delays. When going up for more than a 15 (second delay), you should check into the "winds aloft". You can always check the jumpers ahead of you and compare their exit points with their opening points, call aviation weather, and you can always ask the pilot prior to exit if he senses any changes in the winds aloft. Above 9,500', compensate .4 kms (¼ mile) for each 24 kph (15 mph) of wind. Below 9,500', cut the correction in half. The affect of the winds aloft on your fall will depend on how much time you take. Falling slow, spread and stable, you will drift further than in a full delta.

The selection of the exit point will also be affected by the amount of "forward throw". As you exit, you are traveling the same speed as the jump ship and are thrown forward. Your trajectory is dependent mostly upon the speed of the aircraft at the time you leave the step and it is considerable. For example, from twelve grand at 110 kts, a 175 lb. jumper will be thrown 1,500' (460m).

"Exit lag" must also be cranked into the computations. If you are making a door exit by yourself, there is no lag and you can forget this part but a poised exit may take you .2 km (⅛th mile). For a group of 3 to 4 strut hangers allow .4 km. At 60 kts, the plane will travel that far in just 12 seconds.

Forward throw and exit lag may be cranked in together because they are in the same direction. For jumps over 9,500', shorten the spot .2 kms for forward throw. For lower jumps use .1 kms. Now you have it: the "cut point". Get the aircraft over here and follow your plan.

On large relative loads, don't compensate, spot the base over the exit point. Everyone else on the load will be flying back to the base.

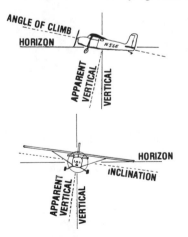

Make sure the plane is flying level.

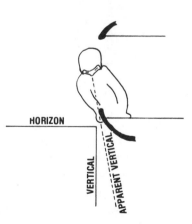

Don't use the side of the plane as a reference point.

Now that you can calculate the cut point, the next task is to direct the jump ship over it. First you must learn to look straight down. This is especially important just before you call for the cut because there is no more time to call for course corrections. And where is "straight down"? If you cock your head forward during spotting, you may exit too soon, for example.

Check the attitude of the plane. If the nose is high as you approach the exit point, you may be looking too far forward and may exit too soon. If your pilot is flying with one wing low, you may be looking down at an angle and be way off the wind line.

Aircraft climbing

Aircraft descending

Left wing low

Correct

Check the attitude of the plane by comparing the wing tip with the horizon.

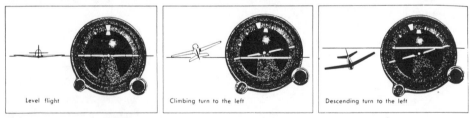

Level flight | Climbing turn to the left | Descending turn to the left

Check the artificial horizon to see if the plane is straight and level.

Glance at the artificial horizon and the needle-ball indicator in the instrument panel. If they aren't centered, bring them to the pilot's attention and ask him to "level the wings".

Don't use the side of the aircraft as a reference point. If it is curved, you probably won't be looking straight down. Keep the corrections small, in five degree increments. Big ones

"Some people spot 'em as they see 'em, some people spot 'em as they are, but there is no spot until you step out the door; and by then it really doesn't matter anyway" — Lynn Levengood

almost always require a banking turn and it takes a while to get the plane back to level. The pilot will try to make uncoordinated, flat (skidding) turns to help keep you oriented. Stick your head out, look straight ahead at the horizon and then look down drawing a perpendicular line. Then look at the horizon under the wing and draw a perpendicular line down below you to check your ground progress. Avoid using the aircraft as a reference; the horizon is always level.

Most spotting errors place the jumpers in the air short and too far left. To be safe, go long. Everyone would rather run a little than have to hold, bucking winds and wondering if they are going to be blown past the DZ.

Once you have passed the cut point, call "cut!" to the pilot and climb out, your spotting is finished. You don't have time for any further course corrections. You can't spot properly from outside after the cut with the airplane going nose low and people hanging everywhere. Besides, no correction can make much difference at this point.

Spotting sounds complicated and perhaps it is. On any given day one will see a bunch of bad ones.

CANOPY RELATIVE WORK

Canopy relative work, like so many other activities in parachuting, began as a stunt. First practiced in 1976, it was demonstrated to the world at the U.S. National Championships in Tahlequah, Oklahoma. A few months later the author penned a parody article reflecting the growth and growing pains of relative work and illustrated it with a couple of CRW photos he had taken. Some liked the joke, some took it seriously and many decided to try it. The new activity soon caught on and demanded its own place in the sport.

Canopy relative work began with, and was touted as, something for relative workers to do after the skydiving was over but it soon carved its own niche and developed its own following. Jumpers began making jumps and pulls from ten grand for CRW only. They talked about it, they wrote about it, they spread the word and it caught on.

Canopy RW is accuracy with a moving disc and it's relative work in slow motion; many of the basics of freefall RW apply. And the excitement of being in the formation lasts minutes, not seconds.

Like freefall relative work, CRW requires training and practice. The novice should learn one-on-one with a seasoned practitioner.

"The more advanced a canopy is, the more gentle you must be when controlling it" — Charles Shea-Simonds.

CHAPTER VI

PARACHUTING EQUIPMENT

Sport parachutists wear two parachutes, a main and a reserve. The reserve, which may be worn on the back or the chest, is carried along in case the main malfunctions.

Contrary to what you might read in the newspapers, parachutes do function properly practically every time. They aren't 100% reliable, if they were, there would be no need for the reserve. But, like the automobile, there are very few unexplainable mechanical failures. Most malfunctions are due to the "nut behind the wheel", or perhaps, the "monkey in the harness" in this case. Parachute malfunctions can usually be traced to the human element, specifically packing, body position at pull time, poor pre-jump inspection, etc. Consequently, while you will be packing your own main parachute, your reserve will be regularly inspected and repacked by a government licensed parachute rigger. You will undergo a rigid equipment check prior to boarding the jump ship and your instructor/jumpmaster will carefully supervise your static line and freefall progression. The key to success and enjoyment in sport parachuting is knowledge; you will want to learn as much about the equipment as possible right from the very beginning.

The parachute assembly is a train of interrelated parts which are carefully engineered into a chain. To keep the weight and volume to a minimum, each part is made just strong enough (with a safety factor figured in) to handle its share of the opening forces. It is rare to see a load bearing component fail in the sport because the gear is "over engineered" as though it were intended for high speed, heavy military use.

The six major components of the sport main parachute are:
* Pilot chute, with bridle,
* Deployment device: Sleeve, bag, etc. and retainer line,
* Canopy, including suspension lines and risers,
* Harness, including hardware, ripcord pocket, etc.,
* Container, and
* Actuation device: Ripcord, static line, etc.

Initially, you will probably be using government surplus parachute equipment which has been modified for sport use. It doesn't compare at all, with the fancy new gear the experienced jumpers are wearing around the DZ, in style, beauty or function. The equipment is designed to do a certain job and freefall relative work makes different demands than static line jumps. However, and this is comforting, the student gear functions more reliably. This is as it should be since the neophyte is not yet as highly skilled in dealing with emergencies.

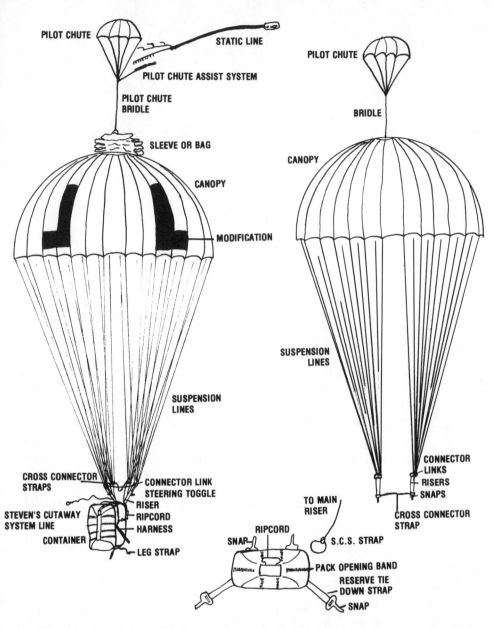

The major components of the conventional sport main parachute. Many student rigs have the Direct Bag system; the bag is attached to the static line and remains with the aircraft.

The major components of the conventional sport reserve parachute. A deployment device may be installed and attached to the apex or the skirt. The canopy may or may not be modified for steerability.

The various components are shown here to acquaint the reader with their location in the complete system. A static line would not be used on a freefall assembly with ripcord while only a dummy ripcord might be found on a static line system. The container is shown closed; it would normally be open with the canopy out.

Riser

Housing

Static line

Break ties or pins in elastic loops

Chest strap
D Ring (reserve attachment)

Reserve ripcord

One type of static line assembly.

Canopy release

Ripcord housing

Main Ripcord

Main lift web

Pack opening, bands

Reserve ripcord

Belly band

Solid Saddle

Typical conventional manually operated assembly.

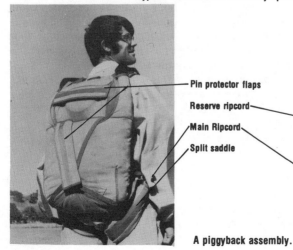

Pin protector flaps

Reserve ripcord

Main Ripcord

Split saddle

A piggyback assembly.

The military surplus equipment must be "modified", or altered, to adapt it for sport use. A deployment device (sleeve or bag) is added to reverse the deployment sequence (lines first) which greatly reduces the forces put on the body during opening. The canopy is modified by removing some fabric and this alteration provides steerability and forward speed while making it more stable. "D" shaped steel rings are added to the main lift webs on the front of the harness so that the reserve may be attached. Two smaller metal rings are sewn to the side flaps of the container for the hooking of the reserve tie down or "belly band". The ripcord and pocket are moved from the left hand main left web to the other to allow a right hand pull. And the top of the container may be altered depending on the type of static line system to be used. A number of things are also altered on the reserve assembly. The snaps are reversed to make attachment easier, the ripcord handle may be moved to a less exposed position, the canopy may be altered for steerability, a Stevens Cutaway System may be installed and an Automatic opener may be attached.

Beyond static line, you will be faced with a choice of reserve mounting; whether to use the conventional back and chest system or the both-on-the-back piggyback assembly. The tandem mount is preferred for relative work as it permits faster tracking, tighter exits, a slower terminal velocity (for more time in freefall) and more subtle maneuvering control. The pig is often used by jumpmasters because the reserve container is mounted out of reach and this makes handling students and static lines simpler and safer. Some of the newer hogbacks are even smaller and lighter than the main parachutes alone of just a few years ago. But many still prefer the conventional assembly which has the reserve in the front where they can see and get their hands on it.

Reserve parachutes must be "approved" under the government's technical standard order (TSO) system either as modified military surplus or through rigid tests on newly designed and manufactured equipment. The main container, risers, canopy, etc., do not have to be "approved" but alterations and repairs may only be made by qualified, licenced people. Minor repairs (those which if done incorrectly would not materially affect the airworthiness of the parachute) may be performed by a licenced senior parachute rigger while major repairs and alterations are reserved for master parachute riggers and parachute lofts.

Jump pilots and observers are also required to wear parachutes in the aircraft but they use regular, unmodified, emergency gear not sport models and they only wear one. The pilot is using the plane as his primary source of transportation and he wears a parachute in case it might fail. The sport parachutist uses the plane as an elevator, a main as his primary source of transportation and a reserve for use if the main fails. Hence the difference.

The deployment of the sport main parachute takes about three seconds. The opening sequence is in the reverse order in which it was packed and is diagramed in chapter two. First, the static line or ripcord is withdrawn unlocking the container. Pack opening bands pull the flaps back exposing the coiled spring pilot chute which jumps out and inflates. The pilot chute "anchors" itself in the air and the jumper continues to fall away. This extends the sleeve or lifts the bag and the lines pay out unstowing from their rubber band retainers, bight by bight. The last stow(s) locks the canopy into the deployment device. When it withdraws, the "trap door" flap opens and the canopy is pulled out. Air rushes into the mouth of the canopy at the skirt and becomes trapped in the top at the apex, filling the canopy. When the canopy achieves maximum width and is nearly full, the jumper comes to a virtual halt and the canopy rebounds inverting briefly and bouncing back up..If a partial inversion malfunction (the most common) is to occur, it happens here when the apex is down and looking for a place to go. Then the canopy reinflates and assumes its steady descent shape.

The sport reserve operates in the same manner unless a deployment device has not been installed or the pilot chute has been removed. The set-up depends on the method of reserve deployment (hand controlled or breakaway) the user subscribes to.

PILOT CHUTE

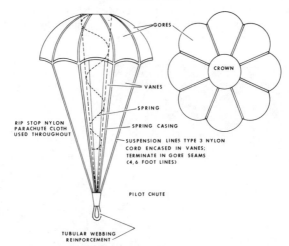

GORES

CROWN

VANES

SPRING

RIP STOP NYLON
PARACHUTE CLOTH
USED THROUGHOUT

SPRING CASING

SUSPENSION LINES TYPE 3 NYLON
CORD ENCASED IN VANES;
TERMINATE IN GORE SEAMS
(4, 6 FOOT LINES)

PILOT CHUTE

TUBULAR WEBBING
REINFORCEMENT

The A-3 spiral spring, vane type pilot chute.

The pilot chute is a small parachute, usually spring loaded, which enters the air stream when released from the packed parachute to act as a drag device and withdraw the canopy from the container, then keeps the lines extended until the main canopy begins to open.

The first man-carrying parachutes were used in balloons and since they were static line operated, a pilot chute wasn't necessary.

With the perfection of the manually-operated parachute in 1919 came a collapsible, spring loaded pilot chute which has been in use now for over fifty years.

The hemispherical, conical or flat octagon, spiral spring vane type pilot chute has proven to be the best design so far. The vanes keep the suspension lines from entangling inside the packed container or catching on feet during deployment as well as decreasing the possibility of inversions. When they are of solid fabric, they cause air to flow into the canopy and when they are of marquisette (mesh) they tend to stop spinning by equalizing pressure. Marquisette is more easily damaged however.

It has been found that an increase in pilot chute area (increased drag) usually improves the dependability and effectiveness of the deployment system. However, larger and multiple pilot chutes also increase the snatch force and add to the stowage problem.

Some modern sport pilot chutes are completely enclosed on the bottom with marquisette.

Many sport parachutists have resorted to installing two pilot chutes to reduce hesitations and speed up deployment. When the dual pilot chute system is added, it is found that they often jump out of the pack in different directions; occasionally one will remain temporarily in the void behind the jumper but it is rare that both do. One or the other nearly always catches air.

Partial inversions and line overs are entremely uncommon when a dual pilot chute setup is used in conjunction with a short sleeve retainer line. The theory seems to be that the two chute arrangement creates more drag and pulls the canopy out faster, loading the system and keeping tension on the main canopy. Additionally, the short tiedown line does not allow the canopy to fall down inside the sleeve during lift off ("canopy slump").

Where two pilot chutes are used, some sleeves and bags should be reinforced and the tensile strength of the tiedown line must be increased. Type III suspension line is sufficient with one pilot chute while, 1,000 lb., ½.. tubular is minimum when using two pilot chutes.

Bag deployed sport canopies have their weight concentrated in one place and present a lifting problem to the pilot chute; duals are a great help here. Larger canopies such as the 35' T-10 normally take a long time to fill. Bag deployment with two pilot chutes will speed it up greatly.

But dual pilot chute arrangements are not for students; they should be used only by those who are pulling stable every time. A horseshoe could result if the pilot chutes were to go around alternate sides of a leg and hang up.

The "throw out" hand deployed pilot chute offers the experienced, stable jumper a number of advantages, the most important of which is reduced pack volume. Stowed in a pocket on the belly band, it doesn't have a spring; you simply pull it out and let it go. This not only eliminates the main ripcord and housing, it permits a small main container. The pack achieves a thinner profile because it doesn't have a coiled spring inside trying to make it thicker.

The reserve may or may not be equipped with a pilot chute depending upon the method of reserve procedure you subscribe to. If you intend to jettison the main (breakaway) before deploying the reserve, then it must have a pilot chute to pull it out of the pack. If you intend to throw out the reserve canopy without jettisoning the main (manually controlled deployment), the pilot chute must be removed from the reserve so that it won't entangle with the main canopy on the way out.

BRIDLE

The bridle, or "pilot chute connector cord" is a piece of line which connects the pilot chute with the canopy or the deployment device (if used). They come in various lengths and strengths and may be either tied on or sewn and looped on. Some experienced jumpers like longer bridles so that the pilot chute is permitted to jump higher before being subjected to a load. Student gear often has a short bridle to reduce the possibility of an entanglement with a foot.

DEPLOYMENT DEVICE

The sleeve   The bag

Deployment devices, sleeves, bags, etc., offer several advantages over straight deployment. They reduce the snatch force of the deploying canopy by reducing its size at line stretch and they tend to save the canopy from damage by making the development more orderly. The system becomes more reliable because the lines pay out and become more evenly loaded prior to canopy inflation.

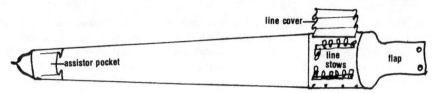

SLEEVE

The sleeve is a long tube of cotton fabric which encases the canopy and reverses the deployment (lines first). It was one of the important basic ingredients which figured in the birth of sport parachuting. Without the availability of inexpensive surplus equipment, its modification for steerability and the use of the sleeve to greatly reduce the opening forces, it is highly doubtful that the sport would ever have appealed to more than a few rugged individualists.

Generally, there are two varieties of sleeves, long and short. Para-Commander class canopies have crownlines; a shorter sleeve may be used and they are stowed back and forth in the top of it.

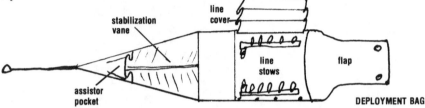

DEPLOYMENT BAG

The bag is more like a pillow case and the canopy is "S" folded from side to side inside of it. Other than that, it is just like the sleeve in that it too reverses the deployment.

Up until just the last few years, the sleeve was far more popular than the bag in sport parachuting. It was easier to pack in outdoor conditions. However, with the revolution in parachute design for relative work and market for smaller, lighter assemblies, the bag has taken over. Used in space and by the military for years, now bags are seen on the DZ as well.

Bags have less weight and volume and further, closing a tight container is easier as they pre-compress the canopy. An additional bonus is that the bag lends a great deal of shaping to the stuffed canopy allowing certain pack stiffeners to be eliminated.

On sport parachutes, the deployment device is tied on and the bag will have a shorter tie on line therefore it won't hang up in the steering slots of the canopy.

Generally, deployment time is faster with a bag while the opening forces may be less than with sleeves. Today, more and more student gear utilizes direct bag static line deployment to take advantage of the positive operating characteristics. In this system, the bag is attached to the static line and is reeled back into the aircraft after use. The military, British X type and U.S. T-10, have been using the system for years.

In Great Britain, after two years and 42,000 direct bag static line jumps, only ten partial malfunctions were experienced and none were serious enough to require reserve deployment.

The POD

The POD (Para Opener Device) from Parachutes Incorporated is like the bag but it splits open and the canopy folds are stacked.

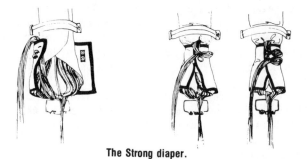

The Strong diaper.

The Diaper from Strong Enterprises wraps around the skirt of the canopy and is locked with a couple of line stows.

The Reuter Wrap from Pioneer encircles the lines and is locked with a pin attached to a short stowed line.

The Slider

The Slider is a rectangle of cloth with a ring in each corner, each of which encircles one of the four groups of lines. It slows the opening by staying up the lines near the canopy restricting its size until the canopy spreads to exert enough force to push the slider down. It not only eases the opening forces, it greatly simplifies packing and is cheap to manufacture.

SLEEVE RETAINER LINES

Note canopy slumped in sleeve.

When the sleeve made its début, it was allowed to float free on deployment; no one thought of tying it on. With the sleeve, the openings were so much more comfortable that jumpers didn't mind chasing, or even losing, the sleeve from time to time.

Extremely short tie down lines tend to slow deployment and may not permit the sleeve to completely lift off of the canopy. On the other hand, extra long lines result in "canopy slump". This occurs as the assembly lifts off of the back and the canopy settles down inside the sleeve. As a result, the canopy emerges from the sleeve in a lump and does not accept the air properly. The time spent in a neat pack job is wasted and the chances of a malfunction are obvious.

The proper solution, then, is a happy medium between the too short and the extra long retainer line. Generally, tie down length is dictated by sleeve width, in that it should be somewhat longer on a relatively narrow sleeve. A three to four foot line seems to be the answer as it keeps the sleeve and pilot chute out of the modification and virtually eliminates the partial inversion when used in conjunction with dual pilot chutes.

Another solution is to switch to a bag, slider, etc.

RISERS

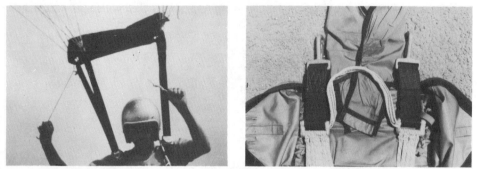

Main risers.   **Reserve risers.**

A riser is a piece of webbing which connects the harness to the suspension lines. Years ago the risers were part of the harness and the lines were sewn directly to the risers. Now the lines are threaded onto connector links and the risers are fitted to the harness with metal riser releases.

The military services developed canopy releases to prevent dragging when landing in high winds but sport jumpers use them to jettison the canopy in the event of a malfunctioned main. Risers on sport rigs are fitted with guide rings for the steering lines and toggles.

CANOPY

The working part of a parachute assembly is the canopy. You are in freefall at terminal velocity hurtling toward terra firma at 190 kph (120 mph), you pull the ripcord and your canopy deploys. Your weight doesn't change but your air resistance does, and dramatically at that. Your new terminal velocity is 17.7 kph (11 mph) and this is a safe landing speed.

Canopies are made of nylon; in the U.S. they have been since 1941 when the Japanese suddenly cut off the silk supply. More recently, the entire parachute, including the container and harness have been made of nylon too.

Most student jumping is done on modified military surplus canopies, usually 28' or 35' in diameter. The larger canopy is heavier and, therefore, a little harder to carry but it also provides more air resistance and descends slower. You will probably be issued a parachute with a 35' canopy if you weigh over 200 lbs. or are over 35 years of age and the modification will be a Double L or a TU.

Some drop zones provide their students with the Para-Commander canopy, a high performance sport canopy with a slower rate of descent. They are more fun to fly but they can get you into more trouble if mishandled so the students usually get a lot of extra training and a radio so they can be talked in.

Before the Para-Commander took over the parachute market in mid 1964 (it dominated almost ten years until the ram airs replaced it), many jumpers purchased new manufacture 28' and 32' flat circular canopies made of a lower permeability ripstop nylon fabric. Since it was new manufacture, it cost more but one also received custom color patterns and a new fabric which provided a lower rate of descent. They were called "low porosity" canopies or "lo-pos". So it wasn't long until the less expensive standard higher permeability military surplus canopy was dubbed the "cheapo".

There are many different weaves, weights, strengths and colors of nylon fabric available for parachute manufacture because of the large sail industry in the United States and the parachute designers are trying them all.

There is a large variety of new equipment but the common surplus canopies are as follows:

The 24' diameter flat circular has 452 square feet of nylon fabric, 24 gores of 4 panels each and 12 continuous lines. Used primarily as a troop reserve, it sees wide spread use in the sport as well. It oscillates badly in its standard configuration and should be modified for steerability and stability.

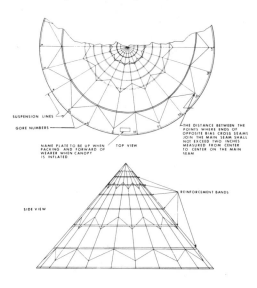

The Strong Enterprises LoPo conical steerable reserve. Note the shape of the canopy.

The 26' Navy conical has 443 square feet of area in a 115.4 degree cone shape and an open diameter of 23.8'. It is like a 26' flat circular canopy with four gores removed providing it with the conical shape. It has 22 gores of four panels each and circumferential reinforcing bands. There are 22 lines terminating just above the skirt.

The 28' flat circular has 616 square feet of area and is similar in construction to the 24' canopy.

The 32' flat circular has an area of 803 square feet and is similar in construction to the 24' and 28' canopies except that it has five panels per gore instead of four. It is not a common size.

The 35' parabolic is the military troop canopy and the largest one common to the sport. Its shape will not allow it to lie out flat on the ground like the 24' and 28' but if it could, it would measure 35' in diameter.

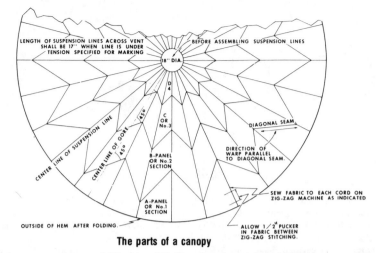

The parts of a canopy

Most canopies are constructed like the 28' flat circular pictured. They are nylon cloth polygons of 28 sides made up of 28 pie shaped gores of four or five panels in each gore and a diameter of 28' when lying flat. The gores are identified with a letter designation starting at the skirt. Bias constructed canopies, which are somewhat stronger and more economical in their use of cloth, are cut and sewn at 45 degrees to the center line of the gore, the same direction as the weave of the fabric. Both the upper and lower lateral bands, the hems at the vent and skirt, are reinforced with a tubular weave nylon webbing to resist tearing. The suspension lines may terminate just above the skirt in some zig zag stitching but many, like the standard 28', have continuous lines, in this case just 14 which rise from the link, pass over the canopy and descend to another link. This forms a strong continuous framework. The Type III line found in the 28' canopy has a minimum tensile strength of 550 lbs. (250 kg).

FRONT

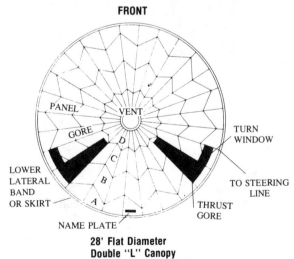

28' Flat Diameter
Double "L" Canopy

The surplus 28' and 35' canopies are altered for steerability. This "modification" results in steerability, forward speed and greater stability and consists of the cutting out of certain areas of the canopy fabric. There are many different patterns in these modifications and before interest turned to the Para-Commander in the sixties, most everything imaginable was tried. Now that the surplus canopies are used mainly for students, all you normally see is a "Double L" in 28' canopies and the same or a "TU" in 35' models.

115

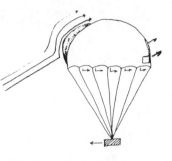

The unmodified canopy.
The trapped air that is not permitted to escape through the fabric, vents, etc. spills out under the lower lateral band causing the load to swing or "oscillate."

The spilling air attaches itself to the sides of the canopy. One side is affected most and moves off center. The load lags and a swinging begins.

The modified steerable canopy. The trapped air is vented in a single direction reducing oscillation and causing glide. Any excess air which may spill under the lower lateral band is forced to slide toward the rear as a result of the relative air flow past the canopy.

The fabric is cut out and the hole is reinforced by binding with nylon tape.

24' TRI-VENT CANOPY

28' DOUBLE "L" CANOPY

28' DOUBLE "T" CANOPY

35' ELLIPTICAL "TU" CANOPY

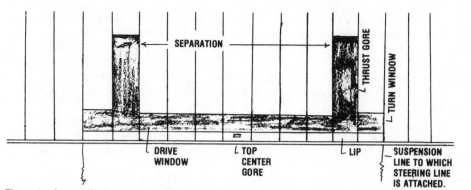

The parts of a modified canopy. The Double L utilizes only thrust gores and turn windows. The TU has drive windows as well.

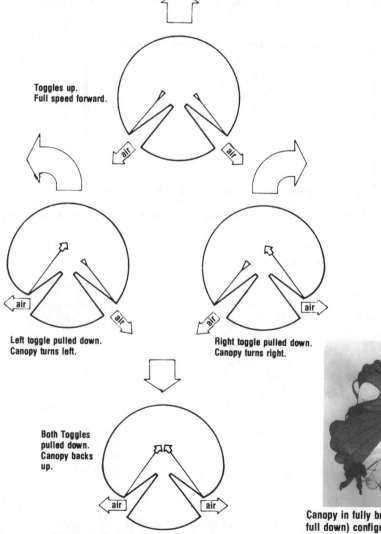

Toggles up.
Full speed forward.

Left toggle pulled down.
Canopy turns left.

Right toggle pulled down.
Canopy turns right.

Both Toggles
pulled down.
Canopy backs
up.

Canopy in fully braked (both toggles full down) configuration.

Steering and braking is accomplished by pulling down on the toggled control lines.

Up to a point, descent rate is lowered once a canopy is modified because the captured air is put to work; it does not spill out under the skirt producing oscillations which drop the load suddenly with each tip. Stability is achieved when enough canopy area is removed to vent the air that would otherwise spill out. Once this point is reached, the removal of more area will only increase the descent rate and, correspondingly, the horizontal velocity. Regardless of the vertical and horizontal speeds, the glide angle always remains the same, usually 38 degrees.

It should also be mentioned that changing the weight of the load within reason will not alter the glide angle, but will change the descent and forward velocity. However, an extremely light or heavy load may alter canopy shaping to the extent that performance is altered.

So a heavier jump will descend faster and have a greater foward speed than a lighter one. Hence, the argument over canopy performance while "running," "holding," "crabbing," etc. Lighter jumpers wishing increased performance should switch to a smaller canopy. Smaller canopies with similar cuts have a greater rate of descent and forward speed but their glide angle is still 38°.

Performance Data Glide Comparison.

Canoy movement in relation to the air.

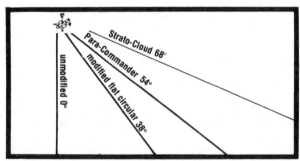

Modified military surplus canopies glide at about 38 degrees. Cutting the holes larger, adding more weight or using a smaller canopy results in greater descent and corresponding forward speed; the angle of glide remains the same.

Generally, sport canopies can be divided into five general classifications: Unmodified, modified, PC class, wings and ram-air.

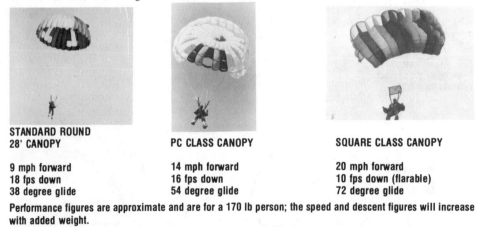

**STANDARD ROUND
28' CANOPY**

9 mph forward
18 fps down
38 degree glide

PC CLASS CANOPY

14 mph forward
16 fps down
54 degree glide

SQUARE CLASS CANOPY

20 mph forward
10 fps down (flarable)
72 degree glide

Performance figures are approximate and are for a 170 lb person; the speed and descent figures will increase with added weight.

"Students should not progress to more sophisticated canopies until they have established a record of safe performance and qualification in standard student equipment" — Russ Gunby.

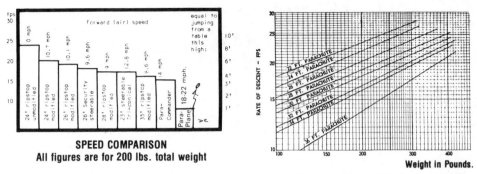

SPEED COMPARISON
All figures are for 200 lbs. total weight

Rates of Parachute Descent for Various Weights.

PARA-COMMANDER CLASS CANOPIES

The Mark I Para-Commander.   The Thunderbow.

This canopy category is named for the PC which dominates it and is characterized by the addition of center lines to pull down the apex. The centerlines spread and flatten the canopy giving it more drag area and a smaller profile. The Mark I PC, the first to be marketed, was far more popular than any of its successors or competitors. Pioneer also built the Mark II, Competition model, Russian PC, RW PC, etc., while other manufacturers produced the Papillon, CrossBow, Starlite and so on.

There are a lot of these canopies around and since most of the more experienced jumpers are opting for the various wings for their better performance and lower weight/volume, there are many on the market at attractive prices. It is always wise to have used gear checked out by a loft prior to purchase and always measure the lines. Many canopies have been "short-lined" to reduce the swing out on turns and lower the weight/volume but using the "more is better" theory, some have been overdone and some have been done twice. So, check them against an original.

> *"Beware of shortlines. Although people always refer to shortlines in terms of 'how much is off the lines', it is 'how much is still on' that counts"* — Gary Lewis

WING CLASS CANOPIES

The Paradactyl canopy.

The wing class canopies are characterized by a single surface airfoil and are very low in both weight and volume. There are only a few wings on the market such as the Delta II ParaWing and the Paradactyl but there are sure to be more in the future.

RAM AIR CANOPIES

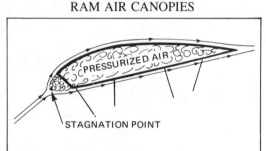

Ram-inflation

Ram Air class canopies have a double surfaced configuration which is inflated by the relative wind to produce an airfoil shape. Their performance is significantly better than round parachutes and they may be "flared" to make the landings very soft. Originally conceived by Domina Jalbert, it was Steve Snyder who put the principles to work and put the canopy on the market.

The Para-Plane. Several versions have evolved to include the Strato Cloud and Strato Flyer.

The Para-Foil. Note the catenary structure on the underside.

The higher performance canopies are closer to airplanes than they are to parachutes and have to be "flown" until the landing is completed. This is quite different from the standard flat circular which will bring you down safely even if you let go of the toggles and cover your head.

RESERVE CANOPIES

Both the law and common sense require the sport jumper to carry an extra "reserve" parachute and while you will be packing your own main, this reserve must be periodically inspected and repacked by a licenced parachute rigger. The reserve must not have a descent rate exceeding 25 feet per second (8 mps) and under 20 is a lot more comfortable. Further, it should be steerable, not only to allow you to pick your landing area but to reduce the oscillation found in uncut canopies. If you weigh less than 175 lbs (80 kg), you may use a 24' canopy, if less than 200 lbs (91 kg) a 26' and if you are heavier, get a 28 footer.

A modified 26' conical surplus canopy

Surplus canopies with diameters of 24', 26' and 28' are often altered for steerability and used for reserves. All three come in a 1.1 oz (max) per square yard ripstop nylon which is characterized by a box pattern weave. Some older 24' models were made of a heavier 1.6 oz twill fabric with a higher permeability. While they are probably still safe, there is some doubt and, in any case, you certainly should not consider purchasing one.

The scarcity of surplus canopies has created a good market for newly manufactured reserves and there are many available.

MID-AIR RESERVE MODIFICATIONS

The "four line release" mid-air reserve modification.

Another approach to reserve steerability is the four line release patterned after the Air Force's mid-air modification to their 28' emergency parachutes. To achieve steerability after opening, the jumper pulls on two lanyards or even cuts the lines to allow the back of the canopy to balloon up. Some people feel that a symmetrical canopy without holes may open more reliably. If so, the four line release certainly provides the best of both the cut and uncut canopies.

HARNESS

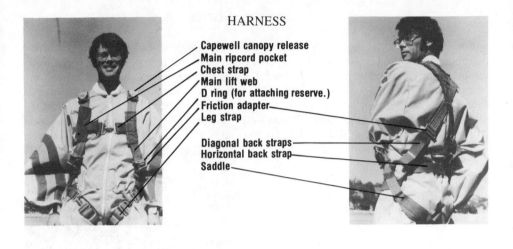

Capewell canopy release
Main ripcord pocket
Chest strap
Main lift web
D ring (for attaching reserve.)
Friction adapter
Leg strap

Diagonal back straps
Horizontal back strap
Saddle

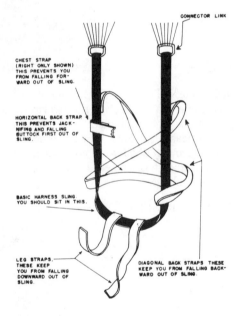

CONNECTOR LINK

CHEST STRAP
(RIGHT ONLY SHOWN)
THIS PREVENTS YOU
FROM FALLING FOR-
WARD OUT OF SLING.

HORIZONTAL BACK STRAP
THIS PREVENTS JACK-
NIFING AND FALLING
BUTTOCK FIRST OUT OF
SLING.

BASIC HARNESS SLING
YOU SHOULD SIT IN THIS.

LEG STRAPS.
THESE KEEP
YOU FROM FALLING
DOWNWARD OUT OF
SLING.

DIAGONAL BACK STRAPS THESE
KEEP YOU FROM FALLING BACK-
WARD OUT OF SLING.

Basic Harness Sling with Supporting Straps Added.

The harness is an arrangement of nylon straps designed to conform to the shape of the body in order to attach it to the canopy and to distribute the opening forces as comfortably as possible. The harness is designed around a sling which takes the greatest part of the opening load. The other straps are added only to keep the jumper from falling out of the basic sling. In fact, the diagonal back straps, for example, take only about 15% of the opening force. Sport saddles may be solid or split and all are very well padded.

CONTAINER

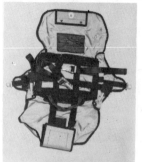

Conventional main container, unpacked.

Chest reserve container, unpacked.

Conventional main container.

Piggyback containers.

Common chest container

POP TOP chest container.

The container or ''pack'' encloses the canopy, deployment device, etc., and is locked closed by a ripcord through a series of cones or loops and grommets. Containers are employed for both mains and reserves and may be mounted on the back or the chest.

The "packtray" is in the base of the container. Unless a deployment device is being used, the lines are stowed here. The container is usually cut on the bias, 45 degrees to the weave of the fabric, to permit a bit of stretch during closing. Containers are not structural members, they simply hang on the harness and hold the canopy.

Container design is simply a question of packaging; where to put so many cubic inches of canopy. All the inside forces pushing out make the container want to assume a spherical shape so some outside forces are needed to push the container back in, to compress it. Tailoring, frames, bows, pack opening bands, etc. are employed. the POP TOP even uses locking strings through the center of the pack to compress it. The NB-6 locks its pilot chute collapsed so that it won't contribute to the internal forces and the new throw out pilot chutes not only eliminate the internal spring, they are mounted elsewhere; the result is a smaller, thinner pack.

RIPCORD

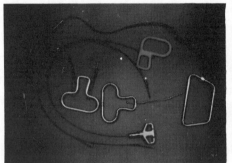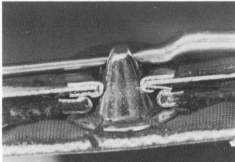

A cutaway view showing the pin locking the stacked grommets on the cone.

The ripcord is a locking device which secures the closed parachute container; it does not open the pack, it simply releases it. It usually consists of a handle (there are many shapes and materials to choose from), a cable of 3/32'', 920 lb. stainless steel, the applicable number of properly spaced pins and a device to attach the cable to the handle such as a swaged (pressed on) terminal ball.

The main ripcord handle is mounted on either the right or left hand main lift web. Most use the right and it is highly recommended as it avoids the cross chest pull which often results in the student going head down on the pull. The left inboard mount was designed for pilots who require a more protected location.

On static line jumps, the ripcord is replaced with a dummy handle. It looks like the real one but does not have a cable and is fitted with a bright colored "flag" so that the jumpmaster can see when it has been pulled. It should also be fitted with some Velcro tape so as to provide some resistance to the pull simulating the friction of the pins in the cones.

Piggyback reserve ripcords are very much like the design for the main but chest pack models have a necessarily shorter cable. The standard military mounting position for the ripcord of the chest mounted reserve is on the right hand side but sport jumpers may move them to the center or other less accessible location to avoid unintentional extraction.

The force required to pull the ripcord will vary quite a bit not only between rigs but between pack jobs on the same rig; you can expect it to be between 2 and 10 kg (5-22 lbs).

RIPCORD POCKET

The ripcord pocket is designed to hold the ripcord in an accessible position. It may be made of fabric, elastic webbing or a steel clip and if of fabric, it may receive its gripping quality from an internal elastic cord or coil steel spring. Certain pockets are made to be compatible with certain ripcord handles.

STATIC LINE

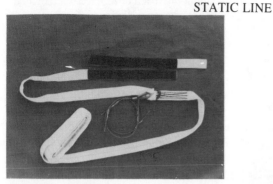

The pin type static line.

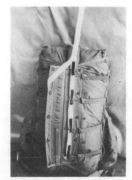

The breakcord type static line, installed.

The static line in use.

After the container is unlocked by the static line, the pilot chute is pulled out by the assist system providing faster deployment.

The static line is a way of attaching the ripcord to the aircraft so that the parachute will be automatically activated as the jumper falls away. It consists of a special locking snap fastener, heavy webbing and either a cable with pins or some breakcord loops. It is fitted with a pilot chute assist system using Velcro or breakcord which pulls the pilot chute from the container after release.

With the direct bag system the arrangement is somewhat different. The deployment bag is attached to the static line and stays with the aircraft.

HARDWARE

Most of the metal fittings on the parachute are forged steel, plated with cadmium to resist rusting. Cones are made of brass and are chrome plated.

Canopy releases were originally designed for the jettisoning of the canopy to avoid dragging in high winds but sport jumpers have adapted them for the breakaway reserve procedure. The older two button and cable models made for the military by the Capewell Manufacturing Co. in Hartford, Connecticut, are being modified or replaced as they had a tendency to hang up and occasionally caught a deploying pilot chute.

L-R: 1750 lb. static line snap, 2500 lb. adjustable quick ejector, 2500 lb. non-adjustable quick ejector, 2500 lb. Air Force leg snap, 5000 lb. Navy reserve snap and 5000 lb. Army reserve snap.

L-R: 2500 lb. D ring, 5000 lb. separable D ring, 5000 lb. angled D ring and 5000 lb. standard D ring.

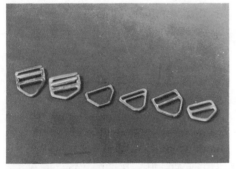

L-R: 2500 lb. deep adjustable V ring, 2500 lb. shallow adjustable V ring, 500 lb. accessory ring, 2500 lb. triangle ring, 2500 lb. deep non-adjustable V ring and 2500 lb. shallow non-adjustable V ring.

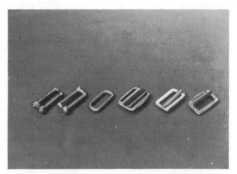

L-R: 3000 lb. speed link, 3000 lb. separable connector link, 3000 lb. solid link, 2500 lb. reversible friction adapter with tensioner spring, 2500 lb. friction adapter, 2500 lb. reversible friction adapter.

The Capewell release. L-R: Lever pin "rivets" and washers, open cable kit, closed cable kit, cable kit installed on female base and male Capewell fitting. 5000 lb. tensile strength.

The Three Ring Circus canopy release in use.

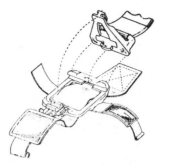
R-3 Canopy release alteration.

Locking cone

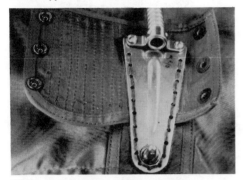
Stiffener with housing, cone and cover.

End tab.

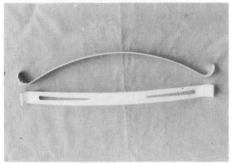
Container bow stiffeners.

Housings.

INSTRUMENTS

There are four ways to determine when you reach pull altitude: stopwatch, altimeter, counting the seconds and eyeballing the ground. Eyeballing is a good backup but it isn't accurate when you are trying to locate a 2,500' mark in the sky. Counting works well on fives and tens but it is difficult to be accurate timing delays of more than ten seconds in this manner.

The stopwatch, usually a 60 second sweep model with a single button, is used to time the planned delay. See the freefall tables in chapter V. The use of the stopwatch is quite simple, e.g., on a twenty second delay, simply punch it as you leave the step and pull when it sweeps past the 20 second mark.

The parts of the altimeter.
A. Aneroid, an evacuated diaphram
B. Rocking shaft assembly
C. Sector gear
D. Calibration arm
E. Diaphram connecting link
F. Handstaff
G. Hairspring
H. Needle
I. Temperature compensator
J. Counterweight
K. Diaphram stop pin
L. Case
M. Opening in case.

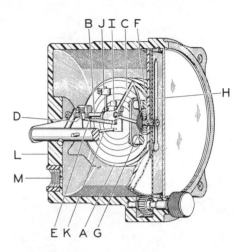

The altimeter operates on an aneroid which is sensitive to changes in air pressure.

The altimeter recognizes and reveals the pull altitude when you arrive there. It has an evacuated chamber called an aneroid which is very sensitive to changes in air pressure. As you descend, the air pressure increases (gets thicker) and the aneroid bends inward. This movement is relayed and amplified through a series of gears and is indicated by a needle on the face of the instrument. The sport models are much smaller and lighter than the standard aircraft equipment. All mechanical devices are subject to failure so you should always check your altimeter against another one. Compare it when you are climbing for altitude; use a friend's or the one in the instrument panel of the jumpship. But be careful: it may be set for sea level. The altimeter is "zeroed" on the ground to calibrate it. If you are planning to land off the DZ, you'll have to find the elevation and compensate for it by adjusting the altimeter. Remember that the altimeter gives you your height above the ground, not above sea level.

| Chest Mount | Harness Mount | Wrist Mount |

The instruments may be mounted on the top of the chest mounted reserve or, if you have a piggyback system, on the chest strap or wrist. Many people prefer a fixed mount reasoning that you can't fly as well if you are constantly pulling in a flying surface (wrist) to see what the altitude is.

Finally, you should practice your count, never put your trust in just one method of altitude assessment and, remember, when in doubt, whip it out!

AUTOMATIC OPENERS

The automatic opener combines a barometric device (similar to an altimeter) and/or a timing device (similar to a watch) with a means of pulling the ripcord of the main or the reserve. Additionally, some have a sensing mechanism which switches the opener on and off so that it fires only if the wearer is descending through 1,000 feet (305 m) at a high rate of speed; there is no need to turn it on and off.

The USPA recommends the use of auto openers, particularly for students, since their statistics show that the devices *might* cut the fatality rate as much as 50%. But everyone, particularly students, must realize that the opener is only a back-up system; they can fail too and should not be relied upon.

There are three types of AODs currently available in North America, the Sentinel Mark 2000, the FXC Model 12,000 and the KAP-3.

The Sentinel Mark 2000.   **The FXC Model 12000.**   **The KAP-3**

The Sentinel Mark 2000 mounts on the reserve parachute, either chest or tandem, and is preset to fire if the user descends through 1,000' at more than 30% of terminal velocity. The most widely used, it has an aneroid, automatic arming sensor and a special ripcord handle with an explosive squib. Prior to each jump, a simple calibration procedure also checks out the circuitry, the battery and the cartridge.

The FXC Model 12000 is barometric, has a rate of descent sensor and pulls the pins with a spring loaded cable. It may be mounted on either the main or the reserve. While somewhat more expensive to purchase, it does not require squib replacement after firing.

The KAP-3 is a barometric and timing auto opener designed for the main parachute. Made in both Czechoslovakia and the Soviet Union, it is in widespread use throughout the eastern European countries. A number have been imported into North America. Completely mechanical, the KAP-3 has proven to be rugged, simple and reliable.

PERSONAL EQUIPMENT

Jumpsuit, helmet, boots, goggles and gloves are some of the personal equipment you will want to consider.

"Why automatic openers? The reason we put students out on static line is that we aren't sure they'll pull their main. So how can we assume they'll pull the reserve?" — Mike Johnson

1920s & 30s. Barnstormer. This one used two parachutes, most did not.

1940s and 1950s. Military jumper. They used football helmets at first.

1960s. Sport jumpers used much borrowed military gear and some designed for the sport.

1970s. The sport jumper's gear is all specially designed for flying.

The parachutist's outer garment was called "coveralls" in the early sixties and that was what it was designed to do; provide warmth, protection and to keep the clothes clean. Into the seventies, it became a "jumpsuit", no longer store bought, they were well tailored, fancy custom made specialized equipment. In the mid seventies, with the great interest in relative work, they became bigger and were dubbed "flying suits".

Today's flying suits are huge. They have a lot of extra fabric under the arms and cords inside to hook over the thumb so that you can pull the suit out by extending your arms. They have great flared bells on the arms and legs and there is enough room inside for the whole team. The reason is for "range"; the relative worker wants more speed range. He wants to

"We are the first generation to have the possibility to fly with our own wings" — Magnus Mikaelson.

be able to go faster, slower and to accelerate and decelerate more rapidly. In purchasing one, make sure the sleeve doesn't cover your ripcord hand; two grand is no place to find that your new jumpsuit is too large.

Large "bat wings", while an interesting discussion topic, can be quite dangerous if they restrict arm movement. Some heavier jumpers use small cloth extensions to help them to equalize their terminal velocity.

You will need a helmet to protect your head during relative work exits, in freefall with colliding jumpers, during opening to save the ears from errant connector links and while landing. Make sure it is one of the approved type, has a secure strap, not just a snap, and is cut high in the back so you can get your head back to look up in freefall.

The main reason for wearing goggles is to keep the eyes from watering up. But they will ward off some of the small things flying around at altitude which could injure the eye. You may not bother with them on static line, someone else will be spotting and you won't be out the door very long. But one cannot perform safe, competent relative work unless he can see clearly. Be wary of large rubber goggles with wide frames, they restrict the peripheral vision and make it difficult to locate the ripcord. Big ones also have a tendency to blow off in freefall. If you wear glasses, there are goggles which will fit over them or you may prefer to wear only the glasses secured with an eyeglass strap. Get clear lenses only and steer away from the other flavors. You'll need all the light you can find jumping late in the day. Visors and face shields are out, they will blow off in freefall.

Gloves provide both warmth and protection to the hands; they should be worn if the temperature at jump altitude is below 4 degrees C (40 F) and remember that the temperature drops at a rate of about 3.7 F degrees per thousand feet. That is 37 F. degrees less at 10,000', it adds up fast. Gloves should be as thin as the temperature will allow and you should use them when practicing your ripcord pulls, reserve procedure, etc.

In the early days of sport parachuting, everyone wore the Army boots just like the airborne without realizing that their missions were different. The paratroops use the parachute for transportation, a means to an end. The sport jumper is interested only in the "means" and has no intention of following the jump with a 40 mile problem. Throughout the sixties, most jumpers wore the imported French Paraboot which has a thick pneumatic sole, good ankle support and fits well if you have European feet. Later, most jumpers switched to lighter footgear perhaps one notch above tennis shoes. You may not hit the drop zone on every jump and you want your feet to be prepared for unimproved landing areas. A thick rubber sole will absorb the "sting" of a hard surface while lacing hooks are absolutely out, they could catch a pilot chute, suspension line, etc.

A small, open, accessible knife should be carried, preferably on the jumpsuit rather than the reserve. A small pocket on the sleeve with a Velcro closure is a good place.

> "See how the wings striking against the air hold up the heavy eagle in the thin upper air, near to the element of fire. And likewise see how the air moving over the sea strikes against the bellying sails, making the loaded heavy ship run; so that by these demonstrative and definite reasons you may know that man with his great contrived wings, battling the resistant air and conquering it, can subject it and rise above it."— Leonardo Da Vinci

FITTING THE PARACHUTE ASSEMBLY

Chest hardware should be 12 inches below chin.

2. Put canopy release or shoulder adapter just below collarbone. Use front adjustments.

5. Space chest strap and hardware. Then tighten as last operation.

4. Tighten back straps.

3. Tighten leg straps.

1. Put sling under buttocks.

Instructions in this figure are general, and apply to the proper fitting of any harness. Follow instructions in the order numbered. If you adjust out of sequence, fit will be poor.

TO TIGHTEN WEBBING SIMPLY PULL THE FREE END.

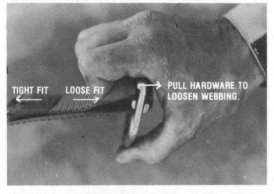

TIGHT FIT   LOOSE FIT   PULL HARDWARE TO LOOSEN WEBBING.

Loosening harness straps.

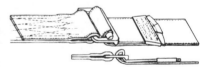

Correct threading of the friction adapter.

QUICK-FIT V RING. TURN ANY QUICK FIT HARDWARE 90° TO WEBBING FOR LOOSENING ONLY.

Quick fit (adjustable) adapters, as found in front and diagonal backstrap adjustments, and quick fit (adjustable) V rings, as found on chest and leg straps, may be easily loosened by pulling on the anvil of the hardware 90 degrees with the fingers, away from the sliding strap. This is easily accomplished even when the harness is on tightly and assembly is under tension. This action faces the hardware so that it will not grip the webbing and the tension on the strap pulls it through the hardware.

Proper harness fit and adjustment is essential for comfort and good flying. Few riggers and fewer users understand the fitting of the parachute and yet it is so very important. A poor fit can take all the fun out of a jump.

The fitting instructions here are written for the standard military surplus Class III harness but are generally applicable to them all. If there are index numbers on the main lift webs, they should be given these preliminary settings:

Height	Index Number
Up to 5'6"	No. 7
5'6" to 6'0"	No. 6
6'0" up	No. 5

Loosen the back, chest and leg straps. Don the harness by placing it over the shoulders. Hook the chest strap but do NOT tighten. Bend over at the waist, reach under the pack and push it up over the shoulders, then slide the saddle down over the buttocks making sure the leg straps are not misrouted. Adjust the main lift webs so that the canopy release hardware is located in the hollow of the shoulders. Hook up the leg straps and tighten them until the saddle is well under the buttocks. Grasp the diagonal back straps and cinch them down. Pull them forward and down to the front until the harness feels snug around the body. The harness should be snug but not so tight you can't walk. Adjust the chest strap. Stow all excess webbing in the elastic keepers provided so that it doesn't flap in the wind.

Now, pick up the reserve and hook it on to the "D" rings on the main lift webs. Get some help and hook the belly band to the small rings on the lower flaps of the main container. Tighten the belly band until the main and reserve are very snug. Stow all excess webbing in the keepers. Now your gear is on and you are ready for the pre-boarding equipment check.

EQUIPMENT CHECK

The equipment check is that all over gear inspection which we conduct on each other prior to boarding the jump aircraft. This final visual and physical pre-jump checkout is not to pass judgement on the design of the equipment, it is a double check on the work of the wearer to insure that he put it on correctly.

The following refers specifically to common surplus equipment with front mounted reserve but it is generally applicable to all parachuting gear. The check should be systematic to insure that nothing is overlooked. It should start in the front, run from top to bottom and then continue in the back from helmet to boots.

The helmet should be tight so it can't slip down over the eyes leaving the wearer "in the dark". Grab the sides and try to rotate it. The strap must be secure, not just a snap on type. Helmets lift off the head easily in terminal freefall and this not only deprives the owner of its protection when he needs it, it presents a danger to spectators below. The canopy releases should be positioned in the hollow of the shoulder, just below the collarbone. If they are the Capewell type, flip the covers, put your hands on them and rotate them outwards so that you can check the mating of the parts as well as for looseness. Replace the covers.

Now moving down, check the chest strap and click the snap. This will reveal a faulty snap or the presence of cloth within the snap itself. Quick ejector snaps demand closer inspection; make sure they are fully seated by pushing the wing closed. Inspect the routing of the chest strap to make sure it is not threaded through the ripcord handle.

Next, pause at the D ring installation seeing that it has been properly done, that the friction adapters are threaded correctly and that the web ends are rolled back and sewn. Click the reserve snaps.

Instruments. Stopwatch wound, both watch and altimeter zeroed. Ask if there is a pilot chute installed, feel for it and check for a ''pilot chute removed'' tag. It makes a difference in the selection of reserve procedure and the wearer may have borrowed this chest pack. Kneel down and firmly grasp the reserve handle in the left hand twisting it gently in its pocket. This action will disclose a tight pocket and, of course, it will be impossible to grasp the handle if there is a pack opening band over it. With the right hand, open the pin protector flap. Pull the handle gently to just barely slide the pins, then grasp the last pin and reseat them. Calibrate the automatic opener per the owner's manual. Check the security of the seal to insure that no one has been inside except a rigger and then look at the packing data card to make sure the reserve is in date. This is primarily to cover yourself in case the FAA shows up. Look at the hooks on the pack opening bands to make sure they haven't worn holes in the container to grab something inside. Count them and check all six ends. Check the position of the instrument panel. Sometimes it is pushed too far forward overlapping the pilot chute and will prevent it from springing out. Make sure the side carrying handles are secured back under a POB so that one won't be grabbed in a hasty search for the ripcord handle. Is the belly band routed properly and secured to the main container?

Now lift the reserve, try to rock it upward; it should be tight. Move on to the leg straps, checking them for trapped fabric. Quick ejector snaps need a comfort pad between them and the jumpsuit. Loose straps should be retained by harness keepers as a loose one may flutter in freefall and this is *very* painful.

Stand back and make an over-all visual inspection of the front. An unzipped leg pocket could put an inexperienced jumper into a spin. If there are lacing hooks on the boots, they must be taped over to prevent them from grabbing errant pilot chutes, suspension lines, etc.

Now, going around to the back, grab the housing and pull it sharply upwards. If it is not the expanding type (from a seat pack), if the cable is long enough, if the housing is secure at both ends, the canopy won't dump out on the ground. Make sure the housing is tacked to the harness within 8cm (3'') of its end to avoid floating ripcords. Make sure the top of the container has been loaded with canopy to provide a firm base for housing-stiffener-pin-cone area. The pin must go straight into the housing or an impossible pull may result. Now grasp the swaged ball on the end of the cable with the right hand and the cable itself above the top pin with the left hand and pull the cable back and forth in a sawing motion. This will reveal kinks, foreign matter such as gravel, etc. Grip the main ripcord handle and wiggle it gently in the pocket. It should be held firmly but not too tightly.

Static line operation requires a couple of extra inspection points. With the pin and cone type, make sure the guide ring is securely fastened to the container and that there is a stiffener between it and the top cone. The cable must be routed through the ring and the pin protector flap should be closed. The breakcord type must not pass through a guide ring and the flap must be left open. Double check the routing of the pilot chute assist system. Inspect the rest of the static line, the snap and the webbing.

''There's more to check than pins'' — Scott Hamilton

Note that the elbow of the pin has snuggled down inside the grommet.

Here the elbow of the pin is resting on top of the grommet.

Open the ripcord pin protector flap. Pins should not be primed more than necessary from the fully seated position but make sure they haven't nested in the grommets. Check for temporary locking pins in elastic loops and under breakcord ties. Close the flap and run the hands over the POBs while visually checking their hooks.

Look at the friction adapters on the diagonal backstraps, you'll find at least one each week that is improperly threaded; check for twists. Make sure the strap ends are stowed so they won't trail and entangle with a pilot chute. Now, a pat on the backpack will signify to the jumper that the check is complete. The whole operation probably took less than a minute.

Once everyone has been checked, equipment should not be removed or altered without a new check. You will want to begin making equipment checks as early as possible in your jumping career to help you learn about your gear. Initially, you will be double checked by your jumpmaster.

This pre-jump routine is often referred to as the "pin check" and this may have to be changed as a lot of the newer equipment uses other methods to secure the closed containers.

PARACHUTE PACKING

The inspection, packing, untangling, carrying and minor maintenance of a sport parachute consumes a large percentage of a jumper's time. Initially, it will take an hour or more to properly pack a main parachute under supervision but as you become more familiar with the packing sequence, this time will be cut considerably.

This section is designed to introduce you to parachute packing in order to help you better understand the operation of your equipment. The parachute is a straight-forward mechanical device yet many people picture it as very mysterious, as though it were guaranteed to fail if not packed absolutely perfectly. The instructions which follow are written for the common Air Force surplus sport assembly but they are generally applicable to all sport rigs.

The parachute rigger seals the reserve after packing.

The main parachute may be packed by an FAA certificated parachute rigger or the user while the reserve may only be packed by a rigger. He also gives the reserve a thorough inspection and when he is finished packing, he applies a lead seal to some safety tie thread and then fills in and signs the packing data card. You will pack your main under supervision until signed off. Prerequisites are the capability to inspect and assess damage, being able to pack, being able to untangle the parachute and the ability to conduct the pre-jump equipment inspection. This will require a considerable knowledge of the parachute and you will probably start your packing just before or just after the first jump.

Tools are not required to pack the sport main but a couple of them will make the job easier. A packing table is not required; most jumpers use a packing mat, swept hanger floor or the lawn.

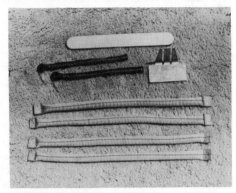 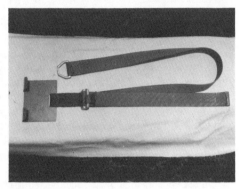

Packing tools: Paddle, flagged temporary locking pins, line separator, shot bags and   a tension board.

The parachute is usually laid out with a packing stake at each end and then stretched tight with a tension board which hooks into the connector links. Most experienced jumpers simply ask someone to put the saddle of the harness around their waist and lean back. But you will use a mechanical device initially as it is doubtful you will be able to find anyone interested in hanging around during the lengthy learning stages.

The line holder neatly secures one group of lines while you are folding the opposite gores of the canopy. The lines are slipped into the ''fingers'' and held in place with a shot bag.

Shot bags are simply weights which hold the canopy and lines in place while you work elsewhere.

A packing paddle may be used to tuck in flaps.

Temporary locking pins are used to secure the container closed prior to the insertion of the ripcord pins. It is very easy to leave them in when installing the breakcord type static line and for this reason, temporary pins should be tied to the packing table or to long red streamers so they cannot be overlooked.

''I prefer to teach packing to the first jump student, in the belief that the more thorough understanding of the equipment gained thereby leads to greater confidence in the equipment and in the student's own competence, which, in turn, may lead to a student whose mind-set is more conducive to remaining in the sport on a long term basis'' — Scott Hamilton

LAYOUT

Stretch the parachute out as if it were being worn and the wearer was lying face down, head toward the canopy. This will place the name plate gore (# 28) and the modified portion of the canopy (rear) up. Hook it up and apply tension. Make sure the canopy is right side out by checking the markings on the name plate panel and the numbers on the "A" panels of the gores. The vent collar should be on the outside of the vent at the apex.

⑦ ⑥ ⑤ ④ ③ ② ①   ㉘ ㉗ ㉖ ㉕ ㉔ ㉓ ㉒

⑧ ⑨ ⑩ ⑪ ⑫ ⑬ ⑭   ⑮ ⑯ ⑰ ⑱ ⑲ ⑳ ㉑

28' canopies

Four line check

Check the lines for continuity. Normally on sport mains, only a "four line check" is necessary. Pick up lines 1 & 14, 15 & 28 at the skirt and walk them back to the links. If they follow to their correct positions, the lines are straight. If the lines check out, you will begin packing. If not, the next task is straightening.

STRAIGHTENING

Canopies sometimes invert or become otherwise entangled on landing. Dips and twists can be terribly frustrating, there may be times when you feel a knife is the only way out. But there are a few tricks in the rigging trade. Always begin straightening at the top. Determine whether the apex is straight by locating and spreading the top center (name plate) gore. Check the printing on the name plate to verify that it is right side out. Follow the gore to the top and straighten the apex. Now count off the gores from the lower lateral band by pleating the canopy. If a tangle is encountered, leave the apex as it is and move the lines and lower portion of the canopy. This may result in further line tangles but that is a problem to be solved later. You should attack the problem in a logical, orderly manner, one step and one area at a time.

If the canopy is completely inverted, reach up inside and pull the apex down and out under the skirt between any two lines. If it's only partially inverted, such as when the harness and lines have passed through one of the canopy slots, it is more difficult. Try to determine how it occurred and pull the canopy back out through the slot. Do it even if this completely inverts the canopy. Then pull the canopy out of the complete inversion as explained above.

Once the canopy is straight, pick up the two top center lines (1 & 28), spread the gore to check for straightness and walk the lines toward the links. If they follow to their proper positions (the insides of the top connector links), the line continuity is probably correct and should be checked and counted off by picking them up in rotational succession and verifying their position on the links.

If they do not check out, remove the links from the tension board and jettison the risers from the harness, if possible.

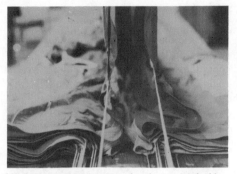

Lift the top center gore exposing the two top inside lines (1 & 28).

Select one of the top center lines and pull on it drawing the riser up to you. This will produce quite a pile of "spaghetti".

Pull the link, riser harness and container through all the lines by routing them over. The point is that now you know the canopy is straight and you know this line is straight.

Stretch the lines back out and repeat the procedure with the other top center line. At this point, the lines will be straight or there will be just a couple of simple dips or twists. Finish with a complete line continuity check.

It should never be necessary to disassemble the connector links to straighten a canopy. It is not likely that the parachute was misassembled and caught only just now. If, therefore, it was right to begin with, you need only reverse the tangling procedure to correct it.

INSPECTION

The sport main parachute should be thoroughly inspected upon original purchase, before placing in storage and, otherwise, on a periodic basis. Briefer inspections take place while packing. You will be looking for wear, stains, missing parts, etc. For a complete, detailed discussion of parachute inspection, see chapter 9 of *THE PARACHUTE MANUAL*.

PACKING

There are many ways to pleat a canopy: one man and two man, right side and left side, each side individually and both to one side. It doesn't matter how the pleating is done as long as the results are correct.

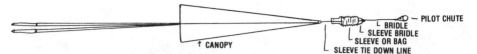

PILOT CHUTE
BRIDLE
SLEEVE BRIDLE
SLEEVE OR BAG
SLEEVE TIE DOWN LINE
↑ CANOPY

1. Layout: Face down, head toward canopy, name plate gore up. (In use the steering slots will face rear.) Inspect thoroughly, checking for damage and completeness, straighten.

SLEEVE   BAG

The sleeve or bag should be bunched up around the apex of the canopy.

Inspect the assembly unless already done as mentioned (Supra); straighten the apex.

Vent collars: Gently pull the vent collar over the upper lateral band and even up the vent. Then gently move the collar back.

No vent collar: Just straighten the vent-hem.

Add more tension.

LINES 1 TO 14   LINES 15 TO 28

The four line check on 28 gore canopy

Grasp the lines just below lateral band, raise and shake vigorously. This will redistribute the canopy fabric back up the lines and eliminate tight panels at the apex. The canopy may have slumped down and while this shouldn't affect deployment, it may affect the neatness and ease of packing.

Spread the two groups of lines to reveal the top center and bottom center gores. Make a four line check.

2. Pleat: In the normal manner with an equal number of gores to each side.

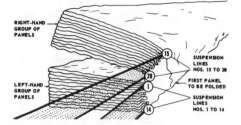

Throw the right side up over the left revealing the bottom gore and line 15.

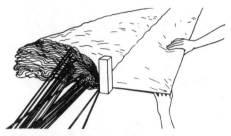

Pull out the bottom center gore.

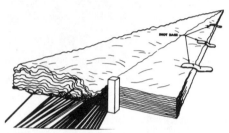

Continue pleating and folding all the gores on that side.

Flip the left side group of gores over the right and pull out the lowest gore.

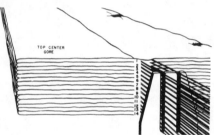

Continue pleating and folding all the gores on that side.

Straightening The Lower Lateral Band.

Pull the canopy off the near side of the packing table and lean on the near side set of gores. Flip the lower lateral bands over revealing the bottom one. Angle this band 90 degrees to the radial seams and straighten the V tab. The V tabs may face up or down but should all face the same direction. Tuck in and straighten the pocket bands, if applicable. Continue until this side is straight.

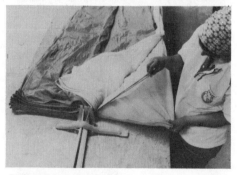

Pull the canopy back onto the table and flip up the other side. Continue straightening the skirt. This method allows all the skirt straightening to be done from one side of the table.

140

3. Fold up 90 degrees so that the lower lateral bands are parallel with the radial seams.

4. Long Fold: To the center and overlapping so that the folded canopy will be the same width as the container.

5. Deployment device.
a. Sleeve: pull down over the canopy even with the lower lateral band.

b. Bag: place the apex in one of the upper corners and "S" fold the canopy into the bag. Push the lower lateral bands straight in.

6. Line stowage: a. Raise the locking flap and make the first stow in one of the upper rubber bands which protrude through the flap.

b. Then lock the other side. The lines should project through the bands between 1'' and 1.5''. Continue stows back down the panel. Close the line cover flap.

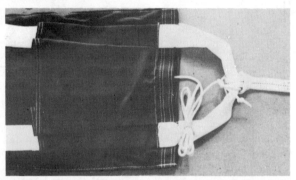

7. Sleeve Tie Down Line Stowage: "Figure eight" the sleeve tie down line into a bunch about 4'' long and stow in a rubber band attached to the sleeve bridle. Excessively long lines may require two bunches.

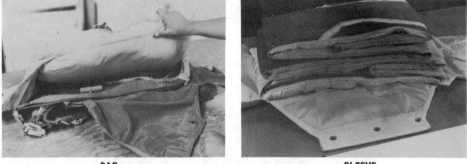

BAG   SLEEVE

8. Skirt End Placement: To the bottom of container. Spread the links in the container.
9. Accordion Folding of Sleeved Canopy: In the usual manner with the first fold a short one. Turn apex under. Actual number of folds depends upon container length. A bagged canopy is already "folded".

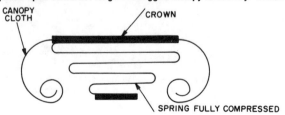

142

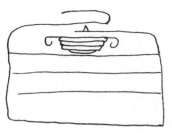

10. Closing: Place pilot chute under the second cone (from the top) and close in the normal manner.
   a. Manual operation: The pins are inserted into the cones in the normal manner.
   b. Static Line Operation:
      1. The assist sysem may consist of Velcro or breakcord. The Velcro type must be well mated. The breakcord type may consist of two turns of 6 cord nylon single or three turns of 6 cord cotton single.

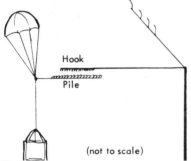

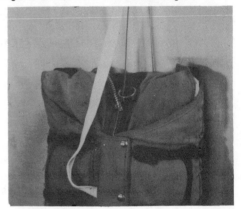

      2. Pin Type
         a. When the container is fitted with standard locking cones, the cable is routed through a guide ring and the pilot chute assist enters the container below the top pin. Snap the pin protector flap closed.

Routing of static line on container with pin and guide ring arrangement.

         b. When the container is fitted with elastic loops, do not route the cable through the guide ring and proceed per the above. Do not snap the pin protector flap closed.

Routing of the static line on container with pin and elastic loop arrangement

3. Breakcord Type. Do not pass the static line through a guide ring. Lay the static line alongside the cones and tie off with two turns of 5 cord or 6 cord cotton or nylon single. An extra turn on the top and bottom cones will guard against premature activation.

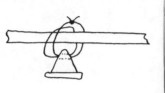

Route the pilot chute assist system into the container below the top pin. Do not snap the pin protector flap closed.

Most containers require a little muscle to close. It will become easier as you learn the tricks.

11. Check the system making certain the pins will be withdrawn or the breakcord will break prior to loading the pilot chute assist system.
12. Dress, inspect and log as required.

    The above is not meant as a complete do-it-yourself packing course; you will be closely supervised when you learn to pack. But this will help you to better understand your gear and will serve as an introduction to packing.

    Packing should be one continuous, uninterrupted operation. Once started, you should not leave the parachute until the packing is completed.

PARACHUTE HANDLING

    Nylon parachutes have only a few enemies: direct sunlight (ultra-violet light), high heat and acid; they should be avoided. Nylon, otherwise, is virtually indestructable. In fact some that are over 25 years old seem to be as strong as the day they were manufactured. The best way to transport a parachute is in a protective bag. Mains are easily carried by putting them on and snapping just the chest strap. Reserve parachutes have carrying handles. For complete rigging and technical information see *THE PARACHUTE MANUAL.*

CHAPTER VII
SPECIALIZED JUMPING

To most people a parachute jump is a parachute jump and it's pretty scary at that. To a seasoned skydiver, there are as many types of jumps as there are ignorant people. He can make low ones or high ones, on land or in the water, at noon or after dark, carrying smoke on a demo or a camera to shoot his friends, singly or with a team, out of a plane or a balloon, practicing for the style event or . . . the list is endless. And, while this book deals with the parachute principally as a means of recreation, it would not be complete without a mention of the other uses. The military airborne troops and the fire fighting smokejumpers use it for quick vertical transportation, military aviators use it as survival equipment and, of course, it is used to drop equipment, to slow race cars, etc. In the next few pages, we will examine some of these uses of the parachute.

NIGHT JUMPS

A "hop 'n pop" after dark.

Night jumps are not only fun to make, they often turn an otherwise dull evening into a great parachuting social occasion. After jumping, it's time to party. Night jumps are more than just an extension of daylight jumping because of the added preparation which is required. One must have lighted instruments, a flashlight to check the canopy after opening, a flashing red light, lighted target, lighted wind drift indicator, additional ground crew, etc. So it is no wonder that night jumps are made less than regularly. Since one 20 second night jump is required for the Class D licence, most drop zones schedule them two or three times a year. For further details on night jumping, consult USPA Part 112.

WATER JUMPS

Water jumps are a great combination of aviation and water sports, something you will want to do at least once every Summer. While unintentional water landings have taken a number of lives, preplanned water jumps have a good record. One water jump is required for the Class D licence and a briefing on unintentional water landings is required for the Class A license. Both planned and unplanned, the jumps terminate in the water. But just like the survival scorecard for each of them, the approach to them is different. In an intentional jump you plan to go into the drink and you prepare for it. You sling the reserve to one side and unsnap all but one leg strap whereas in an emergency dunking you jettison the canopy as outlined in Chapter IV.

Since you are going into the water, you need less protective clothing and want to avoid a big floppy jumpsuit that will make swimming difficult. So you chute up in a helmet, T-shirt, swim suit, tennis shoes (you might miss the lake) and a life vest. Freefall without your familiar jumpsuit will be interesting; there is very little air drag on the extremities and you will probably flail all about trying to grab some air.

After the jump, you will have some equipment to clean and dry. If you went into clean fresh water, the main parachute may be suspended in the shade to drip and dry. The reserve should be taken to a parachute loft for repacking and it is best to leave it in its protective container rather than risk snagging the canopy. If the water was salty, it should be hosed off of the suspended canopy. Neither fresh nor salt water will injure nylon but they will damage cotton so dry out your sleeve or bag right away. Pay special attention to the hardware; dry it so it won't rust.

USPA Part 113 details the best way the experts know to make intentional water jumps. Consult it for further information.

Landing in snow is great fun, especially when it's soft and powdery.

HIGH ALTITUDE JUMPS

The chamber ride teaches each jumper to recognize his own symptoms of oxygen starvation.

Chuted up and ready for a high one.

Most sport jumps are initiated from relatively low altitudes for a number of reasons. Except for the largest team maneuvers, virtually all types of jumping can be adequately performed on a thirty so this 7,200' (2,200m) jump has developed into a standard. The air becomes thinner as you climb higher, airplanes don't run as efficiently so they become more expensive to operate. And in the thinner and thinner air the body falls faster. So you reach a point where a little more altitude just isn't worth the effort.

Most small jump airplanes can't get enough oxygen for their engines when hauling a full load of jumpers above 13,000' (4,000m) and most jumpers begin to notice the effects of oxygen starvation on themselves at about this level. The lack of oxygen (hypoxia) affects each person in a different way but it usually begins with a light headed feeling. Without sufficient oxygen, the brain doesn't operate too well, spotting and other chores become less accurate. So for all these reasons, most high jumps begin at a standardized twelve-five (4,100m) for a sixty second freefall down to pull altitude.

Delay in Seconds	Altitude Meters	Feet	Delay in Seconds	Altitude Meters	Feet
60	3,780	12,400	125	7,620	25,000
65	4,055	13,300	130	8,230	27,000
70	4,420	14,500	135	8,840	29,000
75	4,600	15,100	140	9,450	31,000
80	4,940	16,200	175	10,670	35,000
85	5,275	17,300	180	11,280	37,000
90	5,610	18,400	190	12,190	40,000
95	5,940	19,500	195	13,260	43,500

Because the air pressure decreases with altitude, there is less resistance to the falling body and terminal velocity is higher. This table gives the length of delay from each altitude assuming an opening height of 2,500'.

It is possible to go much higher, we do it all the time but extra equipment is required. Commercial airlines regularly fly at 35,000' to 40,000' (12,000m) with pressurized cabins. If you go above 8,000' (2,500m) for more than 30 minutes, you should have supplimental oxygen aboard the aircraft. In fact, with oxygen, you can go all the way up to 40,000' before a pressure suit becomes necessary. With pressure suits, parachutists have ascended in balloons to more than 100,000' (30,000m).

The temperature also steadily decreases with altitude; just keeping warm can be a big problem.

Physiological flight training is available at several Air Force bases around the country by applying through the USPA and many sport parachutists take advantage of the two day course even if they aren't planning to make a big one. The classroom session is followed by a "chamber ride"; the class enters a large room-size capsule and the air is pumped out to simulate altitude ascension. As they go "higher and higher", each person has the opportunity to observe his own individual reactions to the ever decreasing level of oxygen and then he learns that when he puts on his oxygen mask, it takes only a couple of deep breaths to clear the head and bring him back to normal.

The USPA Doctrine for high altitude jumps is Part 115.

CAMERA JUMPS

Motorized cameras are helmet mounted; the photographer flys in the middle of all the action.

The reason that so many of the aerial photographs in the book are so clear is that they were taken by jumping photographers air-to-air; they were up close to the action. Whuffos, with no understanding of freefall parachuting, often think the photographs were taken from an aircraft (in a 120 mph dive?).

If you would like to get into air-to-air photography, you must be good at both parts, photography and relative work. The first choice will be between still or motion cameras and most select stills because they are cheaper to operate and they allow you to turn from your subject to look at your altimeter in freefall. Some begin with a wrist mounted arrangement but they are difficult to fly with so they soon attach it to the helmet. Most freefall photographers use motor driven 35mm full frame cameras with about a 35mm angle lens and a 1/500 second shutter speed. Those shooting movies use a 16mm gun camera with a wide angle lens. Both are electrically operated, usually with a hand switch.

The best photos are taken on bright days or where there are just a few white cumulus clouds in the background, either early or late in the day when the sun is low. Naturally, light, bright jumpsuits and gear show up better than old dark equipment.

It is difficult to monitor the altitude when shooting pictures and one must be sure to choose reliable subjects who will give him a clear signal at pull time.

A sure way to win friends in parachuting is to buy a camera, the sky above is full of camera hogs.

DEMONSTRATION JUMPS

Demo jumps are great crowd pleasers.

The author is surrounded after landing on a Connecticut beach.

A "demo" jump is one made away from an established drop zone and for the benefit/instruction of the spectators. They are fun to make and fun to watch. The challenge of a good performance into a tight DZ is one that most parachutists will eagerly seek. And, of course, one must be careful to do an especially good job; it's bad press to miss the target.

A good demonstration jump requires a great deal of prior planning from lining up the aircraft with proper radios and pilot to clearing it with the FAA, state and local officials. It is a lot of work to make all the arrangements and get all the required paperwork.

Boot mounted smoke generators accent the fall and aid the spectator in locating the jumpers.

For more information, see USPA's Part 118 Demonstration Jump Doctrine.

MILITARY JUMPING

After basic training in the Army, there are a number of parachuting enlistment options: the Airborne, Special Forces, Rangers, HALO and the Golden Knights.

Airborne training takes three weeks at Fort Benning, Georgia. It takes five static line jumps to earn your wings.

HALO (High Altitude, Low Opening) troops are trained to infiltrate hostile territory by flying over, out of ear shot, and freefalling down to silently open and glide in for a grouped landing behind enemy lines.

The Army Parachute Team, "Golden Knights", consists of two demonstration jump teams and a competition team. They make hundreds of demo jumps each year as part of the Army's recruiting program while the Competition team has produced numerous national and world champions. The home of the USAPT is Fort Bragg, North Carolina.

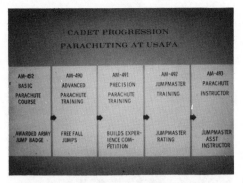

At the Air Force Academy in Colorado, students not only receive a free education, they may learn parachuting for credits.

Low atitude escape sequence.

High speed aircraft require ejection seats for pilot rescue.

SMOKE JUMPING

Heavy protective clothing helps when crashing through trees.

The "Smoke Jumpers", the parachuting firefighters, have become an effective weapon in the constant battle against forest fires.

The parachute was first used to fight fires in 1925 when equipment and supplies were dropped to firefighters on the ground. Time is of the essence when a fire begins and it was later realized that the fastest means of transportation to otherwise inaccessible areas would be via aircraft and parachutes. The time saved in reaching a fire would be measured in DAYS, the amount it cost to fight the fire in thousands of dollars and the amount of land and timber saved in the millions of dollars.

The Forest Service operates a school for smokejumpers at Missoula, Montana. Would-be applicants should be aware that they are more interested in candidates with prior fire fighting experience than seasoned parachutists. In fact, smoke jumping is so different, a sport parachutist finds that many habits have to be broken during training. The Smoke Jumpers, like the Airborne, use the parachute only as quick, efficient vertical transportation.

UNUSUAL JUMPING

After a few jumps, many parachutists become tired of the same old thing and begin to search for ways to diversify their exits, freefall and landings. Here are some of the most interesting variations.

Nine jumpers outside the Fairchild.

Eleven jumpers ride the Beech.

Jumping the Breezy.

Exiting a hot air balloon.

A low level ejection over England.

A Marine bails out with his dog.

A kiss pass.

Owen Quinn goes over the side of the World Trade Center Tower in New York City.

Two Russian acrobats perform as the top man steers the canopy.

Jimmy Davis catches Bobby Ferguson.

A hoop jump.

Bill Ottley releases his seat belt to drop out of this biplane.

CHAPTER VIII
ADVANCEMENT IN PARACHUTING

Many roads to sport parachuting advancement are open to the skydiver and you may wish to pursue one or all of them. Now that you have made your first jump and admit to being hooked, it's time to plan where you are going. There are many avenues and some don't even require jumping participation but all demand dedication to a great sport.

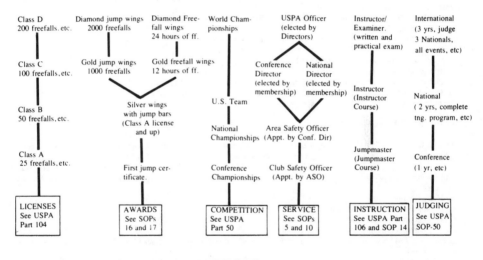

LICENSES	AWARDS		COMPETITION	SERVICE	INSTRUCTION	JUDGING
Class D 200 freefalls, etc.	Diamond jump wings 2000 freefalls	Diamond Freefall wings 24 hours of ff.	World Championships	USPA Officer (elected by Directors)	Instructor/Examiner. (written and practical exam)	International (3 yrs, judge 3 Nationals, all events, etc)
Class C 100 freefalls, etc.	Gold jump wings 1000 freefalls	Gold freefall wings 12 hours of ff.		Conference Director (elected by membership) National Director (elected by membership)	Instructor (Instructor Course)	
Class B 50 freefalls, etc.		Silver wings with jump bars (Class A license and up)	U.S. Team National Championships	Area Safety Officer (Appt. by Conf. Dir)		National (2 yrs, complete tng. program, etc)
Class A 25 freefalls, etc.		First jump certificate.	Conference Championships	Club Safety Officer (Appt. by ASO)	Jumpmaster (Jumpmaster Course)	Conference (1 yr, etc)
LICENSES See USPA Part 104	AWARDS See SOPs 16 and 17		COMPETITION See USPA Part 50	SERVICE See SOPs 5 and 10	INSTRUCTION See USPA Part 106 and SOP 14	JUDGING See USPA SOP-50

LICENSES

The USPA issues four classes of parachuting licenses recognized by all member nations of the Fédération Aéronautique Internationale: Over 13,000 C and 6,000 D licenses have been issued to date. See USPA Part 104 for details.

*104.07 Class A License — Parachutist

Persons who hold a Class A License are certified as able to jumpmaster themselves, pack their own main parachute, and compete in USPA competitions (other than Conference and National Championships). The applicant must have:
    a. Completed 25 freefall parachute jumps including:
        1. 12 controlled delays of at least 10 seconds.
        2. 6 controlled delays of at least 20 seconds.
        3. 3 controlled delays of at least 30 seconds.
        4. 10 freefall jumps landing within 50 meters of target center during which the novice selected the exit and opening points.
    b. Demonstrated ability to hold heading during freefall and make 360 degree flat turns to both the right and left.
    c. Demonstrated ability to safely jumpmaster himself, to include independently selecting the proper altitude and properly using correct exit and opening points.
    d. Demonstrated ability to properly pack his own main parachute and conduct safety checks on his and other parachutist's equipment prior to a jump.
    e. A logbook endorsement by a USPA Instructor/Examiner, a USPA Instructor, his CSO or ASO that he had received training for unintentional water landings.
    f. Passed a written examination conducted by a USPA Instructor/Examiner, USPA Instructor, his CSO or ASO.
    License Fee: $5.00

*104.08 Class B License — Intermediate

Persons who hold a Class B License are certified as able to jumpmasters themselves, pack their own main parachute, are eligible for appointment as Club Safety Officer, and are recognized as having reached the level of proficiency to safely perform relative work and to participate in USPA competitions (other than Conference and National Championships) and record attempts. The applicant must have:
    a. Met all requirements for the Class A license.
    b. Completed 50 controlled freefall parachute jumps (refer to USPA Part 111.08, Progression) including:
        1. 15 delays of at least 30 seconds.
        2. 2 delays of at least 45 seconds.
    c. Demonstrated his ability to complete two alternate 360 flat turns to the right and left (Figure 8) followed by a backloop in freefall in ten seconds or less.
    d. Landed within 25 meters of target center on 10 jumps during which he selected the exit and opening points.
    e. Demonstrated his ability to control and vary both his rate of descent and lateral movement in freefall.
    f. Demonstrated his ability to safely engage in relative work involving at least two jumpers. This includes:
        1) a demonstration of ability to perform acceptable door exits, and
        2) a demonstration of ability to move a horizontal distance away from other jumpers in freefall and check the sky around him so that he may deploy his parachute without danger of collision with a fellow parachutist.
    g. Demonstrated his ability to keep track of other canopies in the air and remain a safe distance from them.
    h. Passed a written examination conducted by a USPA Instructor/Examiner, USPA Instructor, his CSO, or ASO.
    License Fee: $10.00

*104.09 Class C License — Advanced

Persons who hold a Class C License are certified as able to jumpmaster licensed parachutists, pack their own main parachute; are eligible for appointment as Club Safety Officer and Area Safety Officer, are recognized as having reached the proficiency level to participate in USPA competitions (including Conference and National Championships); make relative work, night, water and exhibition jumps; participate in record attempts; and are eligible for the USPA Jumpmaster and Instructor ratings. The applicant must have:
    a. Met all requirements for the Class B License.
    b. Completed 100 controlled freefall parachute jumps including:
        1. 30 controlled delays of at least 30 seconds.
        2. 5 controlled delays of at least 45 seconds.
    c. Demonstrated his ability to perform a controlled international series (Figure 8, Back Loop, Figure 8, Back Loop) in freefall in 18 seconds or less.
    d. Landed within 15 meters of target center on 25 freefall jumps during which the parachutist independently selected the exit point.
    e. Demonstrate ability to ''track.''
    f. Demonstrated the ability to control and coordinate rate of descent and horizontal movement by exiting the aircraft after at least two other experienced parachutists and successfully entering third or later in a star on the same jump.
    g. Passed a written examination conducted by a USPA Instructor/Examiner, USPA Instructor, his CSO, or ASO.
    License Fee: $15.00

*104.10 Class D License — Expert

Persons who hold a Class D License are certified as able to jumpmaster licensed parachutists, pack their own main parachute, may compete in all USPA competitions (including Conference and National Championships); participate in record attempts; make relative work, night, water, and exhibition jumps; are elgiible for USPA Jumpmaster, Instructor, and Instructor/Examiner ratings; and are eligible for appointment as Club Safety Officer or Area Safety Officer. The applicant must have:
    a. Met all requirements for the Class C License.
    b. Completed 200 controlled freefall parachute jumps including:
        1. 100 delays of at least 20 seconds;

2. 50 delays of at least 30 seconds;

3. 10 delays of at least 45 seconds;

4. 5 delays of at least 60 seconds.

c. Demonstrated his ability to perform the following maneuvers on heading in 18 seconds or less (in sequence): Back Loop, Front Loop, Left Turn, Right Turn, Right Barrel Roll, Left Barrel Roll; **or** successfully enter sixth or later in a star which is held for at least an additional 5 seconds or 1,000 feet.

d. Landed within 2 meters of target center on 10 freefall delays during which the parachutist independently selected the exit and opening points.

e. Made one night parachute jump with a delay of at least 20 seconds, with certification of prior night jump training (USPA Instructor/Examiner, USPA Instructor, his CSO, or ASO). Jump must be approved by ASO in accordance with USPA BSRs.

f. Make one intentional water jump with certification of prior intentional water jump training (USPA Instructor/Examiner, USPA Instructor, his CSO, or ASO). Jump must be approved by ASO in accordance with USPA BSRs.

g. Passed a written examination conducted by a USPA Instructor/Examiner, USPA Instructor, or his ASO.

License Fee: $20.00.

AWARDS

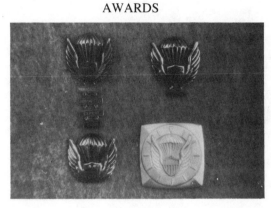

A number of achievements in sport parachuting are recognized by the USPA through a system of awards. See USPA SOPs 16 and 17.

USPA Achievement Award. This is the highest award in American sport parachuting. It is presented only for major contributions in the area of sport parachuting.

First Jump Certificate — Authorized by USPA to be presented by Instructors, and Instructor/Examiners to those persons making their first sport static line parachute jump under the provisions of the Basic Safety Regulations.

Parachutist Badge — Created by the USPA in 1962, a design symbolic of a national aero sport with the wings of flight, the U. S. national shield, and the open parachute. Issued to all license holders. Bars, denoting the particular type of license held, are issued with each new license. Bars are also issued to license holders denoting the number of freefall parachute jumps made; issued in increments of 50.

Gold Expert Parachutist Badge — Awarded to those USPA members holding the US/FAI Class D License who have made 1,000 freefall parachute jumps under the provisions of the Basic Safety Regulations. Must be verified by a Conference or National Director, or by USPA Headquarters.

Gold Expert Parachutist Badge with Diamond(s) — Same requirements as Gold Expert Parachutist Badge, except that the badge has one diamond for 2,000 freefalls or two diamonds for 3,000 freefalls, etc.

Gold Freefall Badge — Awarded to those USPA members holding the US/FAI Class D License who have recorded 12 hours of freefall time, all jumps being made under the provisions of the Basic Safety Regulations. Must be verified by a Conference or National Director, or by USPA Headquarters.

Diamond Freefall Badge — Awarded to those USPA members holding the US/FAI Class D License who have recorded 24 hours of freefall time, all jumps being made under the provisions of the Basic Safety Regulations.

COMPETITION

Competition is an important part of sport parachuting. In fact, some say that you must have competition to call it a "sport". While there are those who enjoy non-evaluated jumping, most get into competition sooner or later, at least at the local level. Many clubs run student events, with slightly modified rules, so you will probably be making competitive jumps very soon.

The "classical", some say "old" events are accuracy and style. Newer team events are four-man and ten-man relative work and these have been modified recently. New ones are eight-man sequential and TRAC (team relative work with accuracy). And a possibility for the near future is canopy relative work.

The 10 cm disc is part of an electronic scoring pad.

Accuracy is the earliest and simplest of the parachuting events. There is very little to it. You exit the aircraft, open and steer to land as close as possible to a 10 cm (3.9") disc. The judges don't bother to measure beyond 10 meters and in national competition, it is normal to have several people tied with ten dead centers after ten rounds. It usually takes a couple of dozen rounds to break the tie. In student competition, accuracy is often modified into a "hit and run" event where the competitor lands as close as possible and then is timed until he steps on the target. This can take quite a while if he lands down wind as he isn't permitted to release his billowing canopy.

Turning good style requires a tight body position.

"Happiness is successfully cutting away a malfunction onto a steerable reserve, at a meet, and coming in for a dead center, standing up; and refusing the rejump" — Mr. Smith

The Style competitor exits the aircraft at 2000 meters (6600'), falls in a tight position for about 15 seconds to build up speed and then whips into a series of maneuvers for time. All three groups are turn, turn, back loop, turn, turn, back loop but there are three combinations. One is right turn, left turn, back loop, right turn, left turn, back loop. Years ago, a time of 15 seconds was good but now you aren't competitive unless you are close to six seconds. And the turns and loops must be good, the judges dock points for undershoots, overshoots and other types of sloppiness.

The Four-Man event begins at 2750m (9,000') and consists of a series of preselected and random formations. If the team completes the sequence within the 35 seconds working time, it begins to repeat the maneuvers.

The Ten-Man speed star was the earliest form of team competition and it drew so much interest that it changed the sport and the competition. In Ten-Man, the team exits the aircraft at 3200 m and puts a ten man star together as fast as possible. In the early days, it was an accomplishment to form a trickily balanced star, now they are being formed regularly in less than 15 seconds.

Eight-Man sequential is a new event and requires the team to exit at 3250 m (11,000') and perform a series of maneuvers, one after the other. Since some of the formations are drawn at random, it is impossible to practice for specific competition. Instead, the teams must do a lot of hot diving and flying to learn to work together and fly well.

The TRAC (team relative work and accuracy) event is for four-man teams. They exit at 2200 m (7200'), make a star, back loop and another preselected formation. Then they are also scored on the accuracy of their landing.

Canopy Relative Work is a new interest and you can expect a competitive event for it before too long. For complete details on competition requirements and events, see USPA Part 50.

There are several levels of competition and you will prove yourself on the local level initially. Beyond the local level, the meets become more standardized and are run by national and international bodies.

The Conference Parachuting Championships is an elimination meet to decide who will go to the Nationals. The U.S. is divided into 12 conference areas.

The National Parachuting Championships chooses the National Champions and selects the U.S. Parachute Team. Men and women compete in separate divisions in the individual events but the team events are mixed.

The National Collegiate Parachuting Championships is for full time undergraduates. Two classes, intermediate and advanced, compete in style, accuracy and relative work.

The World Parachuting Championships are scheduled each year with style and accuracy in the even numbered years and four-man and eight-man in the odd.

Other important international events are the Pan American Cup which is open to the nations in North, Central and South America. They compete in style and accuracy in odd numbered years. The Adriatic Cup is held in odd numbered years in Portoroz, Yugoslavia. It usually consists of accuracy, team and water events. The CISM Meet is for military sport parachutists and is held in even numbered years.

SERVICE

These positions are appointive or elective. For complete details, see USPA SOPs 5 and 10.

Club Safety Officer (CSO) — Responsible for the conduct of safe parachuting operations at a particular club or drop zone. Appointed by the local ASO. May certify Class A Licenses; may certify annual license validation requirements. There are over 100 in the U.S..

Area Safety Officer (ASO) — Responsible for the conduct of safe parachuting operations in a particular geographical area, usually composed of several clubs and/or DZs. Recommended for appointment by the Conference Director. May certify all US/FAI licenses and the Jumpmaster and Instructor ratings. Approves night, water, and exhibition jumps. Certifies annual validation requirements for all US/FAI licenses and the Jumpmaster and Instructor ratings. There are over 200 in the U.S..

Director — A member of the USPA Board of Directors and elected by the USPA membership. Directors meet at least twice annually, serve two-year terms, and may be re-elected.

—Conference Director — Elected by members in the twelve conference areas. Have equal representation with National Directors on the USPA Board of Directors.

> *"One nice thing about our sport of parachuting is that the competitors make the rules"*
> — Eilif Ness.

—National Director — Elected by all the general membership. Represent all the members in USPA ("Ministers without Portfolio"). Usually elected for their ability to make particular contributions to the sport. The Board has ten National Directors.

Officer — Elected by the Board of Directors from among members of the Board. Elected every two years with the seating of each new Board. There are six USPA Officers: Chairman of the Board, President, Vice-President, Secretary, Treasurer, and an at-large member of the Executive Committee.

INSTRUCTION

Competence in the instruction and supervision of students and (when required) other parachutists is assured by a system of three ratings. See USPA Part 106 and SOP 14.

Jumpmaster — Possesses at least a Class C License. May jumpmaster static line and freefall students. Has passed an oral and practical examination, administered by an ASO or Instructor/Examiner. There are over 1,400 currently rated Jumpmasters in the U.S.

Instructor — Holds all privileges of a Jumpmaster. May teach the First Jump Course and give advanced instruction. May give advanced instruction in night, water, high altitude and relative work jumps when so certified. May certify Class A Licenses. There are over 700 currently rated Instructors in the U.S.

Instructor/Examiner — Holds all privileges of an Instructor. Is an expert in all phases of parachuting. Has passed extensive written and practical tests. May certify all US/FAI Licenses and USPA ratings. May supervise night, water, and exhibition jumps. The highest USPA rating issued. There are over 75 currently rated I/Es in the U.S.

JUDGING

Where there is competition, there must be judges; competitive events, by their very nature, require evaluation.

Judges use 10 power telemeters (spotting scopes) and a watch.

There are three levels in judging: Conference, National and International. Before a judge is selected to judge a National Championships, he must complete a judge training program at a previous Nationals. After several years of exceptional work, he may be nominated for the FAI International Judges' List. Judges maintain log books to record the competitions they work and there is a judging committee which constantly monitors their progress.

Others have developed a high level of proficiency in scoring, recording and other support positions.

OTHER FORMS OF RECOGNITION

Other ratings and awards in the field of parachuting are issued by the Federal Government and private groups. These are in addition to the USPA recognition mentioned earlier.

Parachute riggers are licensed by the Federal Government through the Federal Aviation Administration. One may become a Senior Rigger after considerable schooling and a battery of tests, written, oral and practical. After working for three years in the field and packing at least 200 parachutes, he is eligible to take other oral and practical tests to qualify as a Master Parachute Rigger. For more information, see Federal Aviation Regulation, Part 65.

The Star Crest is a series of awards for achievement in relative work established and conducted by Bill Newell in memory of Bob Buquor, the parachuting photographer who was primarily responsible for the development of large star relative work. The basic SCR is issued to anyone who takes part in an eight or larger star for a minimum of five seconds. Very difficult to accomplish in the early days, over 8,000 have been issued to date. Everyone wears this coveted patch. The SCS (Star Crest Solo) is for those who have entered the star eighth or later as this is a bit harder than going out and playing base for a bunch of good flyers. 4,000 have been issued so far. Other variations are the NSCR for night eight-mans, WSCR for female jumps, etc. For information, write Bill Newell, P.O. Box 4277-P., Bakersfield, CA 93307.

The Cross-Country patch may be earned by exiting no higher than 12,500' and at least 6 miles from the disc. You must land within 25' on a round canopy or 10' on a square. For more information on the Cross-Country Award, write Midwest Sport Parachuting Center, 7621-P Pardee Rd., Taylor, MI 48180.

INTERNATIONAL SPORT AVIATION
competition and records

Fédération
Aéronautique
Internationale

Commission
Internationale
de Parachutisme

National
Aeronautic
Association

United States
Parachute
Association

The official national organization of sport parachutists in the United States is the United States Parachute Association (USPA), a nonprofit division of the National Aeronautic Association. It is the official representative of the Fédération Aéronautique Internationale (FAI) for parachuting in the United States and it is the national representative body for parachutists, drop zones, parachute riggers, and the parachute industry. It is the only organization sanctioning sport parachuting competition and records in the United States.

Join the USPA and become part of the great world-wide fraternity of parachuting; get *Parachutist* magazine and find out what's happening. For more information and an application blank, write USPA, 806 15th St. NW #444-P, Washington, DC 20005.

In Canada, write the Canadian Sport Parachuting Association, National Sports Centre, 333-P River Road, Vanier City, Ontario V5Z 2H4.

APPENDIX
THE LANGUAGE OF PARACHUTING.

Study these essential terms until you can not only define them but explain them.

AIRCRAFT: A device that is used or intended to be used for flight in the air.

ALTERATIONS: Changes to the original configuration, such as removal of a gore, installation of D rings, addition of a sleeve, dyeing of the canopy or any other major change to any portion of the parachute from its original manufacturer's specifications.

APPROVED: An item which in its present form has received official certification from the FAA. This approval may be indicated by a TSO stamped on the article or carry a military designation such as NAF, AAF, or AN. Any surplus military parachute has been "approved" at time of manufacture. If the chute is altered such as removing a gore from the canopy, or installing D rings on the harness, adding a sleeve, etc., it is no longer an "approved" parachute.

AREA SAFETY OFFICER: A USPA appointed official who is entrusted with the surveillance of parachuting activities within a specific area.

AUTOMATIC PARACHUTE OPENER: A self-contained device attached to the parachute, other than a static line, which automatically initiates parachute deployment at a preset altitude, time, percentage of terminal velocity, or combination thereof.

AUXILIARY PARACHUTE: FAA: A reserve parachute. British: A pilot chute.

BAG DEPLOYMENT: A container, usually fabric, and usually enclosed in a parachute pack, containing a parachute canopy. Means may or may not be provided for stowage of suspension lines. A pilot parachute lifts a deployment bag away from a parachute pack, causing the suspension lines to be extended before the canopy emerges from the deployment bag.

BASIC PARACHUTIST COURSE: The course of instruction in sport parachuting beginning with the first jump training and progressing through all the novice skills and knowledge needed to qualify for the A License. After suc-cessfully completing the Basic Parachutist Course, the parachutist is fully capable of safe and competent parachuting without a Jumpmaster's supervision.

BASIC SAFETY REGULATIONS: Minimum requirements which are essential for safe sport parachuting activities. Formulated by the USPA.

BATWINGS: Large rigid or semi-rigid surfaces which are attached to the arms and body to decrease rate of descent and increase glide. Prohibited by BSR's, USPA PART 100, 100.29(c).

BREAKAWAY: A jettisoning of the malfunctioned main parachute by activating riser releases and deployment of the reserve. See "Cutaway".

CANOPY RELEASES: Devices which allow immediate release of the parachute canopy. They disconnect the harness main lift webs from the risers. One type is manufactured by Capewell and is sometimes called the "Capewell Release".

CAPEWELL: A hardware manufacturer in Hartford, Connecticut.

CATERPILLAR CLUB: Established by Leslie Irvin for those who have saved their lives with a parachute.

CERTIFICATED: Describes a personnel parachute holding an FAA TSO Certificate. Also used to refer to other FAA-approved parachutes such as government surplus personnel models which were manufactured under military contract.

CLOTH EXTENSIONS: Small triangular pieces of cloth normally sewn into the armpits, between the thighs, etc., to slow the rate of descent during freefall and to increase the glide ratio. These are not "batwings."

CLUB SAFETY OFFICER: A USPA official appointed by the Area Safety Officer. Entrusted with the surveillance of parachuting activities at a specific club or drop zone.

CONTAINER: That portion of the parachute assembly which holds the canopy in place after being folded. This is not to be confused with the term "pack".

CRABBING: Directing the canopy across the line of wind direction.

CROSS PULL: The position of the ripcord handle of a main parachute which is on the left-hand inboard side of the harness. An inboard pull.

CUTAWAY: The cutting of risers or suspension lines to release the deployed canopy while the parachutist is still in the air. Also used interchangeably with "Breakaway".

DELAYED DROP: A live parachute descent where the activation of the parachute is delayed longer than is necessary to clear the aircraft.

DELAYED OPENING: The normal deployment of a parachute, delayed by an automatic device.

DELTA POSITION: A modified stable freefall position made by the parachutist by drawing his arms back near his sides, which results in a head-low attitude and increases his rate of descent and horizontal movement.

DEPLOYMENT: That portion of a parachute's operation occurring from the moment of pack opening to the instant the suspension lines are fully stretched but prior to the inflation of the canopy.

DEPLOYMENT DEVICE: A sleeve, bag, or other device used to reduce opening shock.

DOCTRINE: Principles, policies, and concepts applicable to a subject which are derived from experience or theory, compiled, and taught for guidance. It represents the best available thought that can be defended by reason.

DOOR EXIT: Leaving an aircraft without touching any part of the aircraft outside of the door; made without bracing to achieve a stable fall position.

DROP ALTITUDE: Actual altitude of an aircraft above the ground at the time of release of equipment or personnel.

DROP ZONE: A specified area into which personnel or equipment are dropped by parachute.

DUMMY RIPCORD PULL: A static line training jump wherein the jumper pulls a ripcord handle from the pocket in order to demonstrate his ability to do so.

EMERGENCY PARACHUTE: A certified parachute which is intended for emergency use.

EQUIPMENT CHECK (PIN CHECK): The final visual and physical check made by the jumpmaster on all parachutists prior to boarding.

EUROPEAN PARACHUTING LEAGUE: An affiliate of the USPA which looks after the member's interests in Europe.

EXHIBITION JUMP: A demonstration jump made away from a recognized drop zone for the benefit and instruction of spectators, the sole purpose of which is not a record attempt.

EXIT POINT: That point in the air at which the jumper initiates his parachute jump.

EXPERT PARACHUTIST: The holder of a US/FAI Class D parachuting license.

FEDERAL AVIATION ADMINISTRATION (FAA): The FAA's primary function and responsibility involves control of the nation's air traffic, including the certification of all civil aircraft and engines, licensing of all civil pilots, mechanics, administration of the Federal Aid to Airports Program and operation of the two Federally owned civil airports serving Washington, D.C.

FÉDÉRATION AÉRONAUTIQUE INTERNATIONALE (FAI): A multi-country organization. Governs all aviation sports. Establishes all official aviation records. Governs official international competitions. Operates through a non-profit National Aero Club in each country.

FIELD PACKING: The temporary stowing of the canopy, etc., in the container after a jump, so that it may be more easily transported to the packing area.

FREEFALL: A parachute jump in which the parachute is activated manually by the jumper at his discretion.

FROG POSITION: A modified stable freefall position made by the parachutist without an arch, with the legs slightly bent and the arms in a U position.

GLIDE: The horizontal movement of a descending canopy.

HARNESS: An arrangement of cotton, linen, or nylon webbing which is designed to conform to the shape of the load to be carried in order to secure it properly, so that the opening shock and the weight of the load are evenly distributed during the descent.

HAZARDS, PARACHUTING: Ditches, telephone and power lines, poles, towers, houses, buildings, hangars, automobiles, highways, airplanes, trees over 30 feet in height, water, and any other obstacles or object which could cause death or severe injury to the jumper.

HESITATION (BURBLE): When the pilot chute momentarily flutters in the low pressure area behind the jumper rather than catching air.

HOLDING: Facing the canopy into the wind to minimize ground speed.

HOUSING CLAMP STIFFENER: A metal plate sewn to the top flap of the main parachute container and used to hold the ripcord cable housing in place and to give rigidity to the housing.

INSTRUCTOR: The holder of this rating possesses all privileges of a USPA Jumpmaster and is certified as capable of safely and competently instructing student and novice parachutists in the parachuting skills required to attain the USPA Class A License.

INSTRUCTOR CERTIFICATION COURSE: A course registered with and approved by the USPA conducted to train, qualify, and certify USPA Instructors as outlined by the ICC Guide Book.

INSTRUCTOR/EXAMINER: Possesses all privileges of a USPA Instructor. An I/E is capable of instruction in all areas of parachuting, including accuracy, style, RW, night, water, and high altitude jumps. The I/E is capable of briefing news media and the general public, as well as State and local government agencies, in parachuting.

INSTRUCTOR SEMINAR: A gathering of five or more USPA Instructors and/or Instructor/Examiners to exchange, discuss, and introduce new ideas to develop, improve, or assure the quality of techniques of instruction of sport parachuting.

INTERNATIONAL PARACHUTING LICENSE: An FAI training, competitive, or exhibition parachuting license issued by the USPA to qualified applicants who meet the minimum requirements as set forth by the USPA and verified by a USPA, ASO, CSO, USPA Instructor, or other designated official.

JUMP AND PULL (HOP 'N POP): Pulling the ripcord immediately upon clearing the aircraft (within three seconds).

JUMPMASTER: 1. The parachutist in command of the other parachutists from the time they enter until the time they exit the aircraft; usually the senior man. Also called "jump leader". 2. Holder of a USPA Jumpmaster rating.

JUMPMASTER CERTIFICATION COURSE: A course registered with and approved by the USPA conducted to train, qualify, and certify USPA Jumpmasters as outlined by the JCC Guide Book.

JUMPMASTER WORKSHOP: A gathering of five or more persons who hold the USPA Jumpmaster rating, assembled to exchange and discuss techniques and information to improve and insure the quality and effectiveness of their performances as Jumpmasters.

JUMP RUN: The predetermined flight of the aircraft prior to exit.

LEAD: The jumper around whom the group formation is built.

LINE, STATIC: A line, cable, or webbing, one end of which is fastened to the pack, the other to some part of the launching vehicle; used to open a pack or deploy a canopy.

LINE, SUSPENSION: Cords or webbing of silk, nylon, cotton, rayon, or other textile materials which connect the drag surface of the parachute to the harness. They are the means by which the wearer or weight is hung or suspended from the inflated canopy.

MAINTENANCE: Inspection, overhaul, repair, preservation and replacement of parts, but excludes preventive maintenance.

MAJOR ALTERATION: An alteration not listed in the aircraft, engine, or propeller specifications:
1) that might appreciably affect weight, balance, structural strength, performance, powerplant operation, flight characteristics, or other qualities

affecting airworthiness; or
2) that is not done according to accepted practices or cannot be done by elementary operations.

MAJOR REPAIR: A repair that:
1) if improperly done, might appreciably affect weight, balance, structure strength, performance, powerplant operation, flight characteristics or other qualities affecting airworthiness; or
2) is not according to accepted practices or cannot be done by elementary operations.
The term "major repair" includes replacement of canopy panels, reinforcing tapes, lateral bands, suspension lines, horizontal back straps, and diagonal back straps.

MALFUNCTION: The complete or partial failure of the parachute canopy to effect proper opening and descent. Some malfunctions are: canopy damage, twisted suspension lines, an inversion or semi-inversion of the canopy, a line-over, etc.

MILITARY SPECIFICATION: A procurement specification promulgated by the military agencies and used for the procurement of military supplies and equipment.

MINOR ALTERATION: An alteration other than a major alteration.

MINOR REPAIR: A repair other than a major repair. "Minor repair" includes such operations as replacing canopies, containers, pack opening bands, cable housings, dual mounting plates, automatic ripcord releases, harness assemblies, repairs to containers, repair of stitching, replacement of harness hardware where major stitching is not required, and ripcord pockets, patching holes in canopies, etc.

MODIFICATION: 1) A change. 2) Often refers to the removal of canopy area to achieve steerability and forward glide.

NAS 804: National Aircraft Standards number 804, which covers minimum performance and safety standards for parachutes to be used in civil aircraft.

NATIONAL AERONAUTIC ASSOCIATION: The Aero Club representing the FAI in the U. S. The USPA is a division of the NAA.

NATIONAL COLLEGIATE PARACHUTING LEAGUE (NCPL): An affiliate of the United States Parachute Association. Supports and encourages parachuting as a collegiate sport;

assists collegiate parachutists in gaining recognition and support of their school; conducts an annual national collegiate parachuting championships.

NIGHT JUMP: A parachute jump made from one hour after official sunset to one hour before official sunrise.

NOVICE: A parachutist trainee who has progressed to the aerial phase of training, but who has not qualified for a USPA Class A License.

OPEN BODY OF WATER: A body of water in which a parachutist might drown upon landing.

OPENING POINT: The ground point of reference over which the parachutist should open his parachute to enable him to drift to the center of the target area.

OPENING SHOCK: The force felt by the jumper when the canopy opens. It is affected by velocity, atmospheric conditions, body position, type of canopy, method of deployment, etc.

OSCILLATION: The swinging of the body under the canopy. Caused by air spilling under the skirt. Occurs in turns, etc.

OUTBOARD: Facing to the outside, such as a ripcord facing to the side of the jumper rather than toward the breast bone.

PACK: Such as back pack or chest pack, means the parachute assembly less the harness. That is, it means the container, canopy, suspension lines, pilot chute, risers and connector links. The term "pack" and "container" are not synonymous.

PACK TRAY: The portion of the container or deployment device in which the lines are stowed.

PARACHUTE: A device designed to trap a large volume of air in order to slow the descent of a falling load attached to the parachute. The word "parachute" is formed from the French words "para", shield, and "chute", fall. Thus, "parachute" literally means "to defend from a fall".

PARACHUTE, FREE TYPE: A parachute which is not attached to an aircraft but is operated by the jumper at his discretion.

PARACHUTE, PILOT: A small parachute used to accelerate deployment; constructed in much the same manner as the main canopy and from similar material. Some types of pilot chutes are equipped with a spring-operated, quick-opening device. The frame is compressed so as to open immediately when released from the pack.

PARACHUTE, STATIC LINE OPERATED: A parachute operated by a length of webbing after a jumper has fallen the length of the static line. The ripcord pins are pulled from the pack, or the "break cord" breaks, freeing the parachute.

PARACHUTIST: A person engaging in intentional parachuting such as a sport parachutist, member of a military airborne unit, or smoke jumper.

PARTIAL INVERSION: A type of deployment malfunction. It occurs when one or more gore sections near the skirt become inverted during deployment and form a small pocket which inflates, causing a partial inversion of the canopy. The condition may or may not work out or may become a complete inversion; i.e., the canopy turns completely inside-out. It is the skirt, not the line, which is "over"; not to be confused with a "line-over". Also called a "Mae West".

PILOT CHUTE ASSIST SYSTEM: A connection of breakcord, Velcro, etc., between the static line and the pilot chute of a sport parachute which pulls the pilot chute out of the pack and then separates.

PLFs (PARACHUTE LANDING FALLS): The method of falling down on landing by which the jumper resists, absorbs and distributes the landing forces over various muscular parts of the body rather than on just the legs.

POISED EXIT: A departure from an aircraft wherein the jumper uses any external structure to brace himself and to assist in gaining a stable position immediately as he leaves the aircraft.

POROSITY: The ratio of void or interstitial area to total area of a cloth. Expressed in percent. Used for ringslot, ribbon, ringsail, rotofoil and sport-modified canopies.

PREMATURE OPENING: Opening of a parachute before the user is clear of the aircraft; any accidental opening of a parachute.

RELATIVE WORK: Aerial maneuvers by two or more free-falling parachutists in order to form a star, etc.

RESERVE PARACHUTE: The second or "auxiliary" parachute worn by a person making an intentional jump.

RESERVE STATIC LINE: Line attached to main parachute riser and to reserve ripcord handle to effect automatic opening of the reserve following breakaway.

RUNNING: Directing the canopy down wind to maximize ground speed.

SPLIT SADDLE: The lower part of a harness which has independent leg straps, no saddle cross strap.

SPORT PARACHUTIST: One who engages in parachuting as an avocation rather than as a vocation or duty.

SPOT: The exit point.

SPOTTING: Selecting the course to fly, directing the pilot, and selecting the correct ground reference point over which to leave the aircraft.

STABLE FALL POSITION: A position attained by the free-falling parachutist in which he makes only controlled, preplanned movements. Usually face to earth.

STABILITY: That property of a body which causes it, when its equilibrium is disturbed, to develop forces or movements tending to restore the original condition. (not "Z"; or unstable).

STATIC LINE: A line attached to the aircraft and to the parachute which initiates deployment of the parachute as the load falls away from the aircraft.

STATIC LINE JUMP: A parachute jump during which deployment of the parachute is initiated by means of a static line attached to the aircraft, used primarily in student training.

STUDENT: A parachutist trainee in ground school who has not made a sport parachute jump.

"T" TYPE: U. S. Army description for troop or training parachutes.

TARGET (DISC, PEA GRAVEL, "PEAS"): The prepared landing area.

TECHNICAL STANDARD ORDER: U. S. Government Regulations applying to standards of materials and products. Parachutes are covered by TSO-C23.

TERMINAL VELOCITY: The greatest speed at which a body falls through the air (14.7 psi). Resistance to the air (your size) overcoming the pull of gravity (your weight) establishes the approximate figure of 176 feet per second (120 mph) which is reached after the 12th second of freefall.

TRACKING: A position assumed by the freefalling parachutist in order to attain maximum horizontal drift.

USPA BOARD OF DIRECTORS: Those officials elected by the general membership of the USPA every two years as set forth in the USPA By-Laws; authorized by the By-Laws to have general charge and control of the affairs, funds, and property of the organization; shall carry out the objectives of the organization and its By-Laws; elects officers from among current Board members. The USPA Board of Directors shall consist of:
a) National Directors — those Directors elected at large by the general membership; and (b) Conference Directors — those Directors of a specified geographical area, elected by and responsible for representing the interests of the parachutists of his Conference area.

USPA JUDGE: A parachuting official appointed by USPA for a specific term. He may act as contest director at competitions and may monitor record attempts for USPA.

UNITED STATES PARACHUTE ASSOCIATION: A non-profit division of the NAA which governs sport parachuting activities in the United States.

WAIVERS: Permission granted by competent authority to deviate from the BSR's. Authority to grant waivers is vested in the Board of Directors, the Executive Committee, and in a few cases, the Area Safety Officer.

WATER JUMP: A parachute jump which is terminated by an intentional landing in an open body of water.

WIND DRIFT INDICATOR: A device used to predict wind drift, so constructed as to descend at a rate comparable to a parachutist of average weight descending under a fully deployed main canopy of average specifications. Usually a weighted strip of crepe paper 10 inches wide and 20 feet long.

WIND SOCK: A pole mounted cloth tube of varying diameter which shifts with the wind changes indicating ground wind velocity and direction.

WHUFFO: A non-jumping spectator. Often heard to say: "Whuffo they jump out of airplanes". A "ground hog".

APPENDIX
FOR MORE INFORMATION

U.S. PARACHUTE CLUBS AND CENTERS

Drop zones are located in or near the following cities and towns. For more information and the exact location, look under ''parachutes'' in the Yellow Pages of the applicable telephone directory and/or visit the airport in the location listed. Groupings are by ZIP Code.

United States Parachute Association
806 15th Street NW #444-P
Washington, DC 20005

01364 Orange, MA
01376 Turners Falls, MA
01433 Ft. Devens, MA
01437 Pepperell, MA
02048 Mansfield, MA
02375 E. Taunton, MA
03033 Brookline, NH
04462 Millinocket, ME
06029 Ellington, CT
06070 Simsbury, CT
06238 Coventry, CT
07703 Ft. Monmouth, NJ
08048 Lumberton, NJ
08701 Lakewood, NJ

10996 West Point, NY
11940 E. Moriches, NY
12056 Duanesburg, NY
12095 Johnstown, NY
12525 Gardiner, NY
12582 Stormville, NY
12953 Malone, NY
13054 Durhamville, NY
13148 Seneca Falls, NY
13303 Ava, NY
13795 Kirkwood, NY
14082 Java Center, NY
14172 Wilson, NY
14464 Hamlin, NY
15426 North East, PA
15690 Vandergrift, PA
15530 Berlin, PA
17344 McSherrystown, PA
17550 Maytown, PA
18053 Germansville, PA
18222 Drums, PA
18413 Clifford, PA
19525 Gilbertsville, PA
19966 Millsboro, DE

21660 Ridgely, MD
21795 Williamsport, MD
22134 Quantico, VA
22471 Hartwood, VA

Other organizations which may be
contacted through the USPA include:
National Parachute Riggers' Association
Drop Zone Owners & Operators Association
Parachute Equipment Industry Association

22960 Orange, VA
22980 Waynesboro, VA
23181 West Point, VA
23434 Suffolk, VA
23521 Little Creek, VA
24084 Dublin, VA
25701 Huntington, WV
27549 Louisburg, NC
28107 Midland, NC
28307 Ft. Bragg, NC
28365 Mt. Olive, NC
28376 Raeford, NC
28456 Rieglewood, NC
29078 Lugoff, SC
29461 Moncks Corner, SC
29632 Clemson, SC

30161 Rome, GA
30240 LaGrange, GA
30549 Jefferson, GA
30720 Dalton, GA
31313 Hinesville, GA
31905 Ft. Benning, GA
32034 Fernandina Beach, FL
32077 Palatka, FL
32351 Quincy, FL
32544 Hurlburt, FL
32720 Deland, FL
32726 Eustis, FL
32780 Titusville, FL
33030 Homestead, FL
33456 Indiantown, FL
33579 Sarasota, FL
33599 Zephyrhills, FL
33842 Haines City, FL
35150 Sylacauga, AL
35462 Eutaw, AL
35804 Huntsville, AL
35902 Gadsden, AL
36083 Tuskegee, AL

36360 Ft. Rucker, AL
36530 Elberta, AL
37083 Lafayette, TN
37118 White House, TN
37166 Smithville, TN
37659 Jonesboro, TN
39111 Magee, AL
39773 West Point, MS

40004 Bardstown, KY
40507 Lexington, KY
42071 Murray, KY
42223 Ft. Campbell, KY
44074 Oberlin, OH
44080 Parkman, OH
44231 Garrettsville, OH
44460 Salem, OH
44837 Greenwich, OH
45068 Waynesville, OH
45122 Goshen, OH
45385 Xenia, OH
46158 Mooresville, IN
46731 Craigsville, IN
47166 Ramsey, IN
47610 Chandler, IN
47978 Rensselaer, IN
48463 Otisville, MI
48813 Charlotte, MI
49068 Marshall, MI
49286 Tecumseh, MI

50220 Perry, IA
50659 New Hampton, IA
50651 LaPorte City, IA
53051 Menomonee Falls, WI
53104 Bristol, WI
53120 East Troy, WI
54020 Osceola, WI
54729 Chippewa Falls, WI
54880 Superior, WI
54963 Omro, WI
55081 Stanton, MN
55927 Dodge Center, MN
57039 Lennox, SD
58051 Kindred, ND
58271 Pembina, ND
59714 Belgrade, MT
59901 Kalispell, MT

60034 Hebron, IL
60520 Hinckley, IL
61021 Dixon, IL
61234 Annawan, IL
61554 Pekin, IL
61938 Mattoon, IL
62049 Hillsboro, IL
62246 Greenville, IL

62286 Sparta, IL
63090 Washington, MO
64067 Lexington, MO
65251 Fulton, MO
66092 Wellsville, KS
66442 Ft. Riley, KS
67501 Hutchinson, KS
68061 Tekamah, NE
68531 Lincoln, NE
68847 Kearney, NE

70433 Covington, LA
71459 Ft. Polk, LA
72024 Carlisle, AR
73044 Guthrie, OK
73069 Norman, OK
74070 Skiatook, OK
74464 Tahlequah, OK
74501 McAlester, OK
75069 McKinney, TX
75218 Dallas, TX
76309 Wichita Falls, TX
76528 Gatesville, TX
76544 Ft. Hood, TX
77006 Houston, TX
77573 League City, TX
77706 Beaumont, TX
78230 San Antonio, TX
78653 Manor, TX
79106 Amarillo, TX
79416 Lubbock, TX
79604 Abilene, TX
79924 El Paso, TX

80026 Lafayette, CO
80135 Sedalia, CO
80477 Steamboat Springs, CO
80840 USAFA, CO
81224 Crested Butte, CO
81611 Aspen, CO
83201 Pocatello, ID
83221 Blackfoot, ID
83350 Rupert, ID
83647 Mt. Home, ID
83669 Star, ID
83801 Athol, ID
83843 Moscow, ID
84013 Cedar Valley, UT
84074 Tooele, UT
84321 Logan , UT
84409 Ogden, UT
84770 St. George, UT
85041 Phoenix, AZ
85228 Coolidge, AZ
85344 Parker, AZ
85635 Sierra Vista, AZ
86322 Camp Verde, AZ

87103 Albuquerque, NM
87108 Albuquerque, NM
88002 White Sands, NM
89030 N. Las Vegas, NV

92010 Otay, CA
92330 Elsinore, CA
92370 Perris, CA
93268 Taft, CA
93501 California City, CA
93941 Fort Ord, CA
94509 Antioch, CA
94535 Travis AFB, CA
94550 Livermore, CA
94567 Pope Valley, CA
95531 Crescent City, CA

95616 Davis, CA
96021 Corning, CA
96113 Herlong, CA
96734 Kaneohe, HI
96786 Schofield Barracks, HI
97378 Sheridan, OR
97405 Eugene, OR
97501 Medford, OR
98027 Issaquah, WA
98290 Snohomish, WA
98443 Ft. Lewis, WA
98591 Toledo, WA
98953 Zillah, WA
99352 Richland, WA
99507 Anchorage, AK
99701 Fairbanks, AK

CANADIAN PARACHUTE CLUBS AND CENTERS

Drop zones are located on or near the following cities and towns. Visit the airport in the location listed.

Canadian Sport Parachuting Association
National Sports Centre
333-P River Road
Vanier City, Ontario K1L 8B9

BRITISH COLUMBIA
Abbotsford
Chilliwack
Comox
Kelowna
Terrace
Prince George
Victoria
Kamloops
Williams Lake
Quesnel

ALBERTA
Claresholm
Cold Lake
Andrew
Edmonton

SASKATCHEWAN
Regina
Saskatoon

MANITOBA
Gimli

PRINCE EDWARD ISLAND
CFB Summerside

ONTARIO
Welland
Orillia (Coldwater)
Picton
Sudbury
Winchester
Simcoe
Thunder Bay
North Bay
CFB Petawawa
Gananoque
Arthur

QUEBEC
St André Avelin
Rouyn
Bellefeuille
St-Thomas de Joliette
St-Antoine du Richelieu
Valcourt
Alma
St-Honoré
Victoriaville
St-Jean Chrysostome
Rivière-du-Loup
Baie Comeau

NEW BRUNSWICK
CFB Gagetown
St John
Fredericton (Blissville)

NOVA SCOTIA
CFB Shearwater
Waterville
Sydney
Trenton

NATIONAL PARACHUTING ORGANIZATIONS

Argentina: Fed. Argentina de Paracaidismo, Anchorena 275-P, Buenos Aires.
Australia: Australian Parachute Fed., P.O. Box 21-P, Doveton, Victoria. 3177
Austria: Aeroklub, Prinz Egen Strasse 12-P, A-1040 Wein.
Canada: CSPA, Nat. Sports Centre, 333-P River Rd. Vanier City, Ontario.
China: R.O.C. Parachute Assn., 434 Ke-Nan St. Taipei, Taiwan.
Danmark: Dansk Faldskaerms Union, Idraettens Hus, Brondby Strand 20-P, DK-2600 Glostrup.
France: F.F.P., 35-P Rue St. Georges, Paris 9e.
Germany: Deutscher Aero Club c.v., Lyoner Strasse 16-P, D-6000 Frankfurt/Main 71.
Great Britain: BPA, 47-P Vaughan, Leicester LE1 4SG.
Indonesia: AVES SPC, Djuanda 262-P, Bandung.
Ireland: Irish Aviation Club, Dublin Airport.
Japan: U.S. Forces in Okinawa and Iwakuni.
Korea: U.S. Forces in Camp Humphreys.
Mexico: Club Para. de Mex., Annillo Perriferico y Ave. Conscripto, Mexico 10, D.F.
The Netherlands: K.n.v.V.L.A.P., St. Martinuslaan 124-P, Voorburg.
New Zealand: NZ Para. Fed., P.O. Box 21-016-P, Auckland 8.
Norway: Norges Lufsportforbund, Nedre Slottsgate 17-P, N-1 Oslo.
Panama: Coco Solo and Panama R.P.
Philippines: PPF, P.O. Box 276-P, Makati, Rizal D 708. And, U.S. Forces in Cubi Point and Clark Air Base.
South Africa: Aero Club, P.O. Box 2312-P, Johannesburg.
Spain: FENDA, c/o Ferraz No. 16-P, Madrid
Sweden: SPA, KSAK, P O Box 1212-P, S-11182 Stockholm.
Switzerland: Aero Club, Lidorstrasse 5-P, CH-6006 Lucerne.
USA: U.S. Para. Assn., 806 15th St. NW #444-P, Washington, DC 20005.
Venezuela: Para Club Caracas, Apartado 80016-P, Caracas 108.

In other countries, check with the national aero club.

PARACHUTING EQUIPMENT COMPANIES

Parachutes Incorporated
P.O. Box 96-P
Orange, MA 01364
(Catalogue $1.50)

National Parachute Supply
RD #6-P, Fairview Drive
Flemington, NJ 08822
(Free brochure)

USPA Store
806 15th St. NW #444-P
Washington, DC 20005
(Free brochure)

The RW Shop
Rt #13, Box P
Brookline, NH 03033
(Catalogue $1.00)

The Chute Shop
Hwy #202-P
Flemington, NJ 08822
(Free catalogue)

Strong Enterprises, Inc.
11236-P Satellite Blvd.
Orlando, FL 32809
(Catalogue $1.00)

Barber's Para Sales
423-P Center Street
Manchester, Ct 06040

Sport Chutes & Co.
365-P Atlantic Street
Buffalo, NY 14212

Ed Henderson
273-P Gentilly Park
Auburn, AL 36830

Para-Flite, Inc.
5801 Magnolia Ave.
Pennsauken, NJ 08109
(Free brochures)

Parachute Service
447 Mapleview Drive
Buffalo, NY 14225

Mid-Ohio Parachute Co.
6969 Worthington-Galena Rd.
Worthington, OH 43085
(Catalogue $1.00)

Parachute Associates Inc.
P.O. Box 811-P
Lakewood, NJ 08701

Dave DeWolf
VA Clinic, Room 350-P
3rd and Walnut
Harrisburg, PA 17108
(Rigging School)

The Jump Shack, Inc.
45620 Twelve Mile Road
Novi, MI 48050

Midwest Parachute
46901-P Grand River
Novi, MI 48050

Wisc. Parachute Service
W. 192 N. 4944-P One Mile Rd.
Menomonee Falls, WI 53051

Para-Gear Equipt. Co.
3839-P Oakton
Skokie, IL 60076
(Catalogue $1.00)

Sky Sports, Inc.
RR #2, Box P
Hutchinson, KS 67501

Janousek's Lincoln Para Loft
929-P Furnas Ave.
Lincoln, NE 68521

Up and Down Shop
8515-P Eden Valley
Dallas, TX 75217

McElfish Parachute Serv.
2615-P Love Field Dr.
Dallas, TX 75235
(Free catalogue)

The Swoop Shop
2225-L Elmond #P
Austin, TX 78741

Golden Parachute Sales
2404-P Osceola Street
Denver, CO 80212

North West Aero Sports
P.O. Box 441-P
Mt. Home. ID 83647

Parachute Enterprises, Inc.
2627-P Nido Way
Laguna Beach, CA 92651

Parachuting Publications
P.O. Box 4232-P
Santa Barbara, CA 93103
(Free brochure)

The Altitude Shop
927-P Tennessee Street
Vallejo, CA 94590

Stevens Paraloft
9925-P San Leandro St.
Oakland, CA 94603

Pete's Para Equipt. Sales
3632-AP Porter Loop
Schofield Barracks, HI 96557

Armo's Pig Pen Para. Sales
220 Fourth Street #1-P
Ashland, OR 97520

Woodward's Para Sales
2617-P 271st Street SE
Issaquah, WA 98027

Northwest Aero Sports
6478-P Guide Meridian
Lynden, WA 98264

Parachutes Australia
407-P Kent Street
Sydney, NSW 2000
Australia

Southern Cross Parachutes
P.O. Box 21-P
Doveton, Victoria 3177
Australia

Para-Tech Inc.
500-P Sauvé Street West
Montreal, PQ H3L 1Z8
Canada

Niagara Parachutes Ltd.
P.O. Box 927-P
Niagara Falls, Ont. L2E 6V8
Canada

Horizon Aero Sports
1359-P Kingsway
Vancouver, BC V5V 3E3
Canada

Para-Fun International
Nørrebrogade 148-P
DK-2200 København N.
Danmark

Holstein Marketing Org.
Gershøj Havnevej 12-P
DK-4050 Skibby
Danmark

Geelan & Hughes Ltd.
11-P Westlake Place
Sutton Benger
Chippenham, Wilts.
·Great Britain

Parachutes and Para Equipt.
15-P Waiapu Road
Kelburn, Wellington
New Zealand

KATO Marketing A/S
Postboks 2731-P
St. Hanshaugen
Oslo 1
Norway

P.I.S.A.
P.O. Box 33077-P
Jeppestown, 2043
South Africa

Para-Centro Locarno
Aeroporto Cantonale (P)
CH-6596 Gordola-Locarno
Switzerland

BOOKS

Write for latest price and delivery information or see your local parachute dealer. There are scores of books on the sport of parachuting so only the most recent and most valuable are listed here.

Gregory, Howard. *Parachuting's Unforgettable Jumps*. Howard Gregory Associates (P.O. Box 66-P, La Mirada, California), 1974. A historical view of both airborne and sport parachuting.

Gunby, R. A. *Sport Parachuting*. Denver: Jeppesen and Company, 1972. A basic handbook of sport parachuting.

Keech, Andy. *Skies Call*. Andy Keech (6339-P31st Place N.W. Washington, D.C.), 1974. Outstanding photos by a gifted sport parachuting photographer.

Kittinger, Joseph W., Jr., and Caidin, Martin. *The Long, Lonely Leap*. New York: E. P. Dutton & Co., Inc., 1961. Detailed account of Kittinger's historic jump from 102,800 feet.

Mackersey, Ian. *Into the Silk*. New York: W.W. Norton & Company, Inc., 1958. A story of the Caterpillar Club with descriptions of unusual emergency parachute jumps.

Poynter, Dan. *Parachuting Manual with Log*. (Parachuting Publications, P.O. Box 4232-P, Santa Barbara, CA 93103). A basic text for the novice.

Poynter, Dan. *Parachute Rigging Course*. (Parachuting Publications) A course of study for the FAA senior rigger certificate.

Poynter, Dan. *I/E Course*. (Parachuting Publications) A home study course for parachuting Instructor/Examiner candidates.

Poynter, Dan. *The Parachute Manual*. (Parachuting Publications) A technical treatise on the parachute of special interest to parachute riggers.

Rankin, William H. *The Man Who Rode the Thunder*. (Englewood Cliffs, New Jersey: Prentice-Hall, Inc., 1960). A description of Colonel Rankin's emergency bailout from 50,000 feet into a thunderstorm that kept him in the air for 40 minutes.

Ryan, Charles W. *Sport Parachuting* (Henry Regnery Co., Chicago) An illustrated guide to parachuting.

Sellick, Bud. *Parachutes and Parachuting*. Englewood Cliffs, New Jersey: Prentice-Hall, Inc., 1971. An illustrated description of modern sport parachuting.

Shea-Simonds, Charles. *Sport Parachuting*. (London, Adam and Charles Black). A popular text on British parachuting.

USPA Instructor's Handbook by the USPA Safety and Training Committee, available only through the USPA Store. A booklet of articles reprinted from *Parachutist* magazine. The articles cover a wide range of topics relevant to sport parachuting instruction.

Owner's Manuals, The manufacturers of sport and emergency parachutes also publish manuals that describe details on the use, packing and maintenance of the particular assembly. These manuals should always be read by the owner or rigger of the parachute and they also are excellent sources of accurate and detailed information for the parachuting instructor. Most manuals can be obtained for a small fee (usually about $1) by writing directly to the manufacturer.

PARACHUTING MAGAZINES AND NEWSLETTERS

Write for a sample copy and a subscription blank.

Parachutist Magazine
806 15th St. NW #444-P
Washington, DC 20005
Attn: Mike Leeds, Editor

Para News Hawaii
99-116 Konomua St. #206-P
Aiea, HI 96701
Attn: Joel Salazar, Ed.

Spotter Newsmagazine
654-P Washington Street
Braintree, MA 02184
Attn: Rita Donaldson-Pernaw

L.V. Freefall Forum
4631-P Marnell Drive
Las Vegas, NV 89121
Attn: Harold Acheson, Ed.

Starcrest Magazine
P.O. Box 4277-P
Bakersfield, CA 93307
Attn: Bill Newell, Ed.

Mountain Memo
1357-P East Willow Vista Dr.
Sandy, UT 84070
Attn: Larry Bagley, Ed.

Sherry's Newsletter
11631-P Cimarec
Dallas, TX 75218
Attn: Sherry Schrimsher, Ed.

CPI Newsletter
P.O. Box 953-P
Manchester, CT 06040

Mepa News
805-P 15th St. NW #718
Washington, DC 20005
Attn: Wm. H. Ottley, Ed.

Hot Swoop
2617-P 271st SE
Issaquah, WA 98027
Attn: Jamey Woodward, Ed.

Pelican Pouch
P.O. Box 62-P
Ridgely, MD 21660
Attn: Mike Schultz

Northeast News
74 Donald St. #48-P
Weymouth, MA 02188
Attn: Howard White, Editor

Mid-East Conference News
2011-P S. Dixie Avenue
Kettering, OH 45409
Attn: Ed Mosher, Editor

Relative Wind
P.O. Box 1036-P
Lake Elsinore, CA 92330
Attn: Nanc E. Gruttman, Ed.
■------------------
Canpara Magazine
P.O. Box 539-P, Sta. B
Ottawa, Ontario K1P 5P6
CANADA
Attn: Carol Wightman, Ed.

Maritime Para-News
P.O. Box 33-P
Cambridge Station, NS
CANADA   BOP 1G0

SP. Parachutist Magazine
Kimberley House, 47 Vaughan
Leicester, LE1 4SG
GREAT BRITAIN
Attn: C. Shea-Simmonds, Ed.

Free Fall Kiwi
P.O. Box 3603-P
Wellington
NEW ZEALAND

Australian Skydiver
P.O. Box 21
Doveton, Victoria 3177
AUSTRALIA

Sportspringer Magazin
Am Hasengarten 45
D-3300 Braunschweig
WEST GERMANY
Attn: Uwe Beckmann, Editor

Les Hommes Volants
28 rue de Navarin
F-75009 Paris
FRANCE

Sportparachutist Magazin
KNVvL, Jozef Israelsplien 8
's-Gravenhage
THE NETHERLANDS
Attn: Bert Wijnands, Editor

Faldskaermsspringer
Rosen Krarter 9
DK-2990 Niva
DANMARK
Attn: Preben Thorup, Ed.

Fritt-Fall Magazin
Hernesveien 29
N-8000 Bodo
NORWAY

Svensk Fallskarmssport
Iliongranden 310
S-22371 Lund
SWEDEN
Attn: Lars Kroon, Editor

USPA PUBLICATIONS

Order from the USPA Store, 806 15ths Street NW #444-P, Washington, DC 20005

Order No.	Title	Price
L-1101	USPA Constitution and By-Laws—Part 1	*
L-0201	Definitions—Part 10	.25
L-1310	USPA Affiliated Clubs—Part 20	.25
L-0205	Demonstration Jump Insurance—Part 31	*
L-5001	Competition Rules and Regulations—Part 50	
	Conference and National Championships	.50
L-0206	Disciplinary Actions—Part 75	.25
L-0207	Basic Safety Regulations—Part 100	
	(Part 101, Waivers, on reverse side)	*
L-0209	License Application Form—Part 104	*
L-1400	USPA Parachutist Ratings (includes SOP-14) Part 106	.25
L-0210	Doctrine—General—Part 110	.25
L-0211	Novice Training—Part 111	.25
L-0212	Night Jumps—Part 112	.25
L-0213	Water Jumps, Intentional—Part 113	.25
L-0214	Jumpmaster Safety Checks and Briefings—Part 114	.25
L-0215	High Altitude Jumps—Part 115	.25
L-0216	Methods of Instruction—Part 116	.25
L-0217	Relative Work—Part 117	.25
L-0218	Demonstration Jumps—Part 118	.25
L-0219	Auxiliary (Reserve) Parachute—Part 119	.25
L-0220	Equipment—Part 120	.25
L-0235	Federal Aviation Regulations, Part 105	
	Parachute Jumping—FAR 105	.50
L-0236	FAA Advisory Circular	
	Sport Parachute Jumping—AC 105-2	.50
P-0100	Parachutist Guide Book (All above bound in a	
	folder. All publications required for A,B,C,	
	and D License examinations)	3.50
L-1480	Fundamentals of Instruction (24 pages)	1.00
P-0260	First Jump Packet (Includes First Jump certificate)	
	Available only to Instructors and Instructor Examiners	1.75
L-1325	License Rating Renewal Form	*
L-1422	Jumpmaster Proficiency Card	*
L-1459	Instructor Proficiency Card	*
P-0200	USPA Directory	2.00
M-13	USPA 3-ring vinyl binder	3.25
P-0400	PARAVISUALX Training Aid (18 Posters)	9.50

FEDERAL AVIATION ADMINISTRATION PUBLICATIONS

FAA regulations may be obtained from local FAA offices, most parachute equipment dealers and the Superintendent of Documents.

Part 65—*Certification of Airmen Other Than Flight Crewmembers*. This details the requirements and procedures of becoming an FAA Parachute Rigger.

Part 149—*Parachute Lofts*. Gives requirements for issuing parachute loft ratings and general operating rules for FAA certificated lofts.

Part 91—*General Operating and Flight Rules*. This Part establishes federal regulations for general flight operations in the U.S.

Part 37—*Technical Standard Order Authorizations*. FAR 37 prescribes procedures for obtaining a TSO and other related regulations.

Parachute Rigger Certification Guide (Advisory Circular 65-5A). This booklet gives detailed information on how to apply for an FAA Rigger Certificate. Included are sample questions from the written exam and other useful information.

Use of Oxygen (Advisory Circular 91-8A). This publication gives recommended and required procedures for the use of supplemental oxygen during flight.

Airman's Information Manual, Part 1, Basic Flight Manual and ATC Procedures. Published primarily for pilots, this book contains current information on all aspects of using the U.S.'s airspace and airports. It is useful to the sport parachuting instructor who wants to know the last word on all details of navigation aids, ATC procedures, airspace structure, pilot-controller terminology. Issued four times per year.

PARACHUTING FILMS

Write for descriptive brochure and current prices.

A/V FIRST JUMP COURSE
THIS IS A SPORT?
U.S. Parachute Association
806 15th St. NW #444-P
Washington, DC 20005

SKY CAPERS
MASTERS OF THE SKY
WINGS
PLAYGROUND IN THE SKY
Photo-Chuting Enterprises
12619-P South Manor Dr.
Hawthorne, CA 90250

JUMP!
Bulsh Productions
c/o Ramblers Parachute Centre
15-P Wynnum Road
Norman Park
Brisbane, Queensland 4170
Australia